A Tale of Two Cou[s...]
Cuz Poetry is better to[...]

Dora Blandford
&
Verily 1st Earl of Runnymede

2020

To all the Poetry lovers out there.

To/ my darling favourite cousin
Joanne
    with much love
      Your cousin
        Suzanne
          x — x

Thanks for being there!
      x

CONTENTS

4

It's a sad fact of life, competition is rife,
and composers are no less than keen.
And it's hard to get fame, in the lyrical game,
when you think of the poets' there's been.
But all is not told, of the poets of old,
no wonder their works came to light
In their day they were best, compared to the rest,
because most people then, couldn't write.
There was Byron and Burns, who took it in turns,
in the post "Laureate of the year"
Others too performed feats, like Mansfield and Keats,
and the humorous young Edward Lear.
There was Wordsworth (Old Bill) floats on high (Vale and hill)
In a breeze that was driving him crazy.
Saw a host of mauve frills, wrote he' seen Daffodils
'Cause he couldn't spell "Michaelmas Daisy".
But of great girls and men, who employ a fine pen,
and are using a fictitious name.
I'm afraid it is true, that I only know two,
who have managed to side-line all fame.
So, keep both fingers crossed, for all is not lost,
this 'ere book is a gold mine you see.
It was written by Dora Blandford no less,
and her cousin, the Earl verily.

Verily 1st Earl of Runnymede

1

Time for oneself

Sitting here in the garden on a warm and sunny day,
The washing blowing gently in the breeze.
The water in the pond with fountain, sprays with ease,
Time, its passing by sometimes without a thought.
Where nature grows from seed, I think we ought.
To find time to listen to the birds and other sounds,
We won't be here forever we all are heaven bound.
There are many things that we just take for granted,
And hope that our seeds grow of which we've planted.
Hedgerows, grass, pretty flowers and trees,
Are there to help the birds and the bees.
Nature is wonderful and there for us to see,
Take time and enjoy it's there for you and me.

Dora Blandford

Life's a Road

(The author's take on life)

Life's a road, that's long and tiring,
Upon which, until retiring,
You take with burdens, all and any,
Lay byes few and potholes many,
Journeying without a break,
That's how it is, make no mistake,
And mark my words, you've more to pull,
If honest, fair and honourable,
It's quite a treat, when walking by,
To feel good and, hold your head high,
It's something to be treasured when,
You know you've helped out now and then,
And if you do, your peers and Lord,
Will see you get a just reward,
And that my friend, as you'd expect,
Is something that we call Respect!

Verily 1st Earl of Runnymede

Marmalade

(The author's friend happens to have a taste for marmalade)

Each morning at seven, I unlock the door, and await the arrival of a
welcome rapport.
For indeed 'tis my pleasure, as a host to extend, hospitality to, one
who's such a good friend.
"Hello there" I chirp, every day if not most, "The kettle is boiling, and
I've put in the toast".
Thus, a habit was formed, between like-minded peers, as we've both
eaten breakfast, together for years.
Now reflecting on such, as some of us do, very nice you may add and
pray yes, it is true.
For when knowing one's friend, has a need to be fed, it doesn't cost
much for some butter and bread.
Even less for the tea and the wear on the coaster, the electricity used,
when employing the toaster.
But if anyone thinks handsome profits are made, let them look at how
much, my friend likes Marmalade.
I put out a knife, but he well knows my tune, so he puts it away and he
gets out a spoon.
And we're not talking teaspoons, which don't hold enough, more a
shovel to grab, even more of the stuff.
To scoop a big dollop's his favourite trick, with the aims to ensure, a
layer real thick.
Now my friend's skin's turned orange, the dangers are real, for instead
of a beard he's begun to grow peel.
I tried hiding the stuff, in the garage, the loft, but quickly he found it
and ate as I scoffed.
The greenhouse, the freezer, even under the sink, but he soon sussed it
out, pray he smelt it I think.
I even swapped labels, in the hope he would vie, with the Cherry
preserve that was standing nearby.
But my cunning plan failed, and he soon saw the sham, and on that day
insisted, on having the jam.

4

I'm no miser as such, like most bachelors are, and a typical jam costs a few pence each jar.
But when budgeting weekly, which I do in haste, I have to include his extravagant taste.
So, I now buy in bulk like a prudent Innkeeper, because in the long run it works out much cheaper.
And with thanks to my slide rule and several sums, I'm now buying marmalade, in 5-gallon drums.

Verily 1st Earl of Runnymede

Dear Rory

(The author locates for a friend, one of his long-lost ship mates from his naval days)

With respect your long-lost shipmate, I ran a search to see,
If he was in the data bank, of my brand-new CD,
And I'm pleased to say there are two names, you'll find them both attached,
Which fit your said criteria, and in all respects are matched,
So why not give them both a call, it's cheap thanks to BT,
And soon you'll be exchanging, some tales about the sea,
But before you do, some naval terms, you'll need to cast a thought,
Dispense with words like "Left and Right" it's Starboard and its Port,
The "Galley" is a naval term, where hungry seamen go,
It's the place your shipmates ate their food, and not a boat you row,
The "Capstan" is an anchor winch, so please do not forget,
It's not as you may know it, as a well-known cigarette,
The "Bridge" is the control room, where the Captain keeps a look,
It's not a thing that goes across, a river or a brook,
and finally, some sound advice, though you might already know,
It's more or less, how to address, your mate from years ago,
Not that I'm an expert, as you know I'm just a gaoler,
But me I'd call him Michael, and dispense with "Hello Sailor"

Verily 1st Earl of Runnymede

There is a place, of which I'm fond,
It's down in Boyton, called the Pond!

(Someone purchased a Hot Tub and the author was invited to bathe)

Oh, but this Tub's relaxing,
a small but warming ocean,
A whirlpool where, you meet fresh air,
and waters set in motion,
With coloured lights to soothe sore eyes,
where bubbles come and go,
Most pumped up by the motors,
which are hidden down below,
I know this as I know the sound,
of Air-pump motors humming,
But sometimes with the pumps switched off,
the bubbles keep on coming,
That might strike you as pretty weird,
but me I've got no doubts,
It's when the owner's in the pond,
When he's been eating sprouts!

Verily   1st Earl of Runnymede

The Butterfly

(The author read of how endangered the butterfly has become and, having written the following, sent it to the National Newspapers with hopes they would publish it to bring greater awareness)

In a world of many living things, some huge and others small.
Mother nature made diversity, for the pleasure of us all.
There's bats and gnats, and many birds, which nest high in the trees.
There's ants with wings, and wasps that sting, and also buzzy bees.
There's hornets and mosquitoes, with wings as thin as cloth.
There's locusts and there's midges, and several types of moth.
But of all the many creatures, that habitat, the sky.
There's none we hold more pleasing, than the peaceful butterfly.

Their many shapes and colours, like the swallowtail in blue.
The Tortoiseshell, the Orange-tip, whose numbers now are few.
The Marble white, the Grayling, the Duke of Burgundy.
Which sadly have declined of late, and are so rare to see.
The Hairstreak and the Peacock, both streamlined like a kite.
There's Emperors and Admirals, in purple, red and white.
The Wall-Browns and Gatekeepers, and Mountain Ringlets too.
But none so rich in colour, as the famed Adonis Blue.

Yes, a garden's not a garden, without our flutter friend.
They give us so much happiness, and pleasure without end.
But instead of thoughts contented, I'm harbouring despair.
Whereas once they all were flourishing, now sadly they're not there.
The constant use of pesticides, to satiate man's greed.
Combine with that the fact this world, is not inclined to heed.
And I wonder what mentality, and simply wonder why.
We can't all find, or be inclined, to save the Butterfly!

Verily 1st Earl of Runnymede

A happening during the Eclipse....

(The author was gardening on the day a solar eclipse was due, during the actual eclipse
a perfectly formed, heart shaped leaf fell to his feet, he gave it to her with this)

Silently, without a sound,
It stalled and fell, upon the ground,
My eye was trained, its movement caught,
I downed my tools, and paused for thought,
No title, type, no creed or name,
And so, I looked, from whence it came,
By comparing, and by chances,
Trying all, the local branches,
I could not match, I thought how strange,
Its parent must, be out of range,
I pondered, figured, and contrived,
But could not twig, how it arrived,
My find was clearly, out of season,
But must have had, some valid reason,
Perhaps thought I, supposed to find,
A message meant, me to remind,
I looked again and saw the clue,
Immediately, I thought of you,
How come it fell, before the fall,
The shape, the shape…that says it all!

Verily 1st Earl of Runnymede

Flowers

(A list of wildflowers seen by the author on his
way to the Bluebell woods with his children)

A bluebell fragrant, one of many,
Fair a hand, was picked at will,
In company by just a sprig,
Of purple coloured, Wood Crane Bill,
Red Campions, abundant they,
Uncountable, indeed were lots,
Plus, Wedgewood blue, and autumn gold,
The colours of Forget-me-nots,
Some Spiderwort, but just a few,
A dolly spray, magnolia white,
Mimicking the snowflake shape,
So elegant and trim a sight,
And finally, so fayre a flower,
So, pleasing for my eyes to greet,
And aptly named, inspiring awe,
A dainty sprig of Meadowsweet.

Verily 1st Earl of Runnymede

Waterloo

(An ex Regimental Sergeant Major of the Grenadier Guards and now Prison Officer, confesses to the author that he cannot stop smoking)

A soldier sat reflecting, with an honest hand on heart,
And thought about the battles, in which he'd taken part,
Of his daring and the exploits, in lands across the oceans,
Which brought him much respect, honour, medals and promotions,
And he held his head up proudly, as they did in his brigade,
For they always stood their ground even when they were afraid,
And now he thought how sad that he, his waterloo had met,
In so much he now takes orders, from a little cigarette.

Battalions of soldiers, with colours close at hand,
Thundered to attention, and all at his command,
If he wanted something doing, if he gave someone a task,
All he did was point a finger, he didn't have to ask,
If he wanted some religion, if he had someone to bless,
He never went to church, God would call in at the mess,
But now he does as he is told and quick enough you bet,
When he gets another order, from that little cigarette

A soldier sat reflecting with an honest hand on heart,
And thought about the battles in which he's taken part,
And he wondered if he had the strength although he wasn't sure,
To fight another campaign and taste victory once more,
A battle very personal, one of painful slaughter,
A round of Armageddon, with little room for quarter,
Will he face tobacco bravely, will he stand up to the threat?
Or just keep taking orders. from that little cigarette.

Verily 1st Earl of Runnymede

11

The Tale of a mystical man by Jove
and strange goings on in Mullion Cove

(The author, wearing a clever disguise and advertising a talent for palm reading,
arranged with his cousin Merv to read the palm of his visiting sister Yvonne, who
had no idea who the palm reader was, not surprisingly the Palmist was extremely
accurate in describing her family and circumstances)

Benjamin Beckett had several charms, was an author of books, and
reader of palms,
Was toting for business, having advertised he, sat waiting for customers
on Mullion quay,
His first client came, not much later on, a very nice girl by the name of
Yvonne,
He saw her suspicions, he saw Mervyn smirking, how little she knew,
that the wind-up was working!

Benjamin held, Yvonne's hand and began, I'll tell you he said, as much
as I can,
You are one of five children, just like yonder mister, both you and he,
must be brother and sister,
Though I'm sorry to add, there's not five anymore, one has passed on,
leaving only the four,
& you've got Scottish Blood pumping round in your veins; I think from
your father who worked on the trains!

This poor girl Yvonne, was now such a sight, her hands they were
shaking, her face had gone white,
Her eyelids shot up, with a crash and a ping, like a roller-blind raised, by
an over-tight spring,
He could hear Yvonne thinking, her face was aghast, how could this
stranger, know all of her past,
But the answer was simple, there down by the water, the fact was
Yvonne, had been led to the slaughter!

Benjamin Beckett then added confusion, and summoned his words in a final conclusion,

He said now I know, that your first name's Yvonne, though born a MacGregor, your surname's now John,

He predicted that shortly, whilst still down the dock, Yvonne would be in, for one hell of a shock,

And fair play to the palmist, for undoubtedly he, was as accurate as, any Palmist could be!

The shock was forthcoming, for Yvonne it was then, but not so for Mervyn, for Wyn Faye and Gwen,

Who all knew exactly, the identity, of the mystery Palmist, resembling me,

Conspirators all, and professional at that, at keeping a secret, well under the mat,

Play-acting their roles, and in the right places, and no tell-tale smirks to be seen on their faces!

The secret that was, so professionally guarded, came apart as the shades, and the wig were discarded,

To reveal an acquaintance, of years more a dozen, no lesser a stranger, than just one more cousin,

So I have to pay tribute, and say thanks to the one, without whom none of all this could be done,

From us all in the cast, with disguises long gone, well done to the real star.........................

And that's you Yvonne!

Verily 1st Earl Runnymede

PS: - This was presented to Cousin Yvonne already framed, as that's exactly what you were

13

Swansea Earthquake

Was relaxing on my sofa, when a shaking I did feel.
What was that? I couldn't work it out! Was that even real?
Shocked and disbelieving, I was startled that's for sure.
Wasn't till a phone call said, did I hear that earthquake roar,
Wow I wasn't dreaming, it really was a quake.
The sofa did some bouncing, it really wasn't fake.
The tremor that disturbed me & left me in a state.
That was my experience, of our Swansea earthquake.

Dora Blandford

The Wordsmith

(A self-assessment of the author's ability to compose)

Now here's the problem see,
I, the Bard, lyricist, the laureate, come poet be,
Have stalled, for lack of a decent and versatile plot,
Quite dissimilar to others that I wrote, and have got,
How can that be, I ask myself, for in judgement many,
Have considered my jocularity and able pen, as fly as any,
My ability to be diverse in word now and then,
Being fair, I'd say nine out of ten,
Spelling, the need of thesaurus or dictionary,
Burke's landed gentry or other similar reference, no not me,
Satirical inference, condescension whilst appearing meek,
And gifted in the art of writing tongue in cheek,
Acrimonious in verse, acerbic and knocking,
At least HNC, but with honours in mocking,
Contemptuous in tone, I can cut to the bone,
Scathing and dry, I do better than try,
Invoking and cynical, sneering and haunting,
A dab hand at diatribe, derisive and daunting,
Being cynical, mordant, rubbing salt in the wound,
Three tools of the trade, in which I'm highly tuned,
But I have just one failing, I have to admit,
Without the above . . . . . . I'd have so little wit.

Verily 1st Earl of Runnymede

15

The Tale of Jack and Jill

(The author's ancestry in verse)

I know a Mrs Sidaway from Cardiff if you will,
Although we're now on first names terms, and so I call her Jill,
Her mother's name was Molline, and she tried hard to fix,
The birthdate of her granddad, in 1876,
His name was Henry Thomas, the years he lived were many,
His wife's first name was Mabel, her second it was Benney,
Henry's dad was Benjamin, whose mother couldn't wait,
To baptise him on Christmas day, in 1848,
Her maiden name was Crundall, her first names Mary Ann,
Having given birth to Benjamin, made Tom a happy man,
Tom's father's name was Benjamin, just like his grandson too,
He married Lizzy Beach, in the spring, 1802,
Ben's father's name was Richard, and did well to survive,
Married three days after Christmas, in 1765,
Richard's dad was Samuel, and we're not out of names,
For Richard had a granddad, and his name too was James,
Now James is someone special, and for you a name anew,
He was christened early in the year, of 1692,
His wife was slightly younger, she was Mary Warrington,
But Mary hadn't finished, and she had another son?

His name was also James, and so we have another,
But born in 1719, making him the younger brother,
He was married to Ann Tompkins, although much later on,
And in 1754, she gave birth to her son John,
John lived in the country, very much a farming man,
And got married, like his father, to another girl called Anne,
They had a son called Thomas, a Waggoner by trade,
And so they say a fair amount of money, must have made,
His wife was known as Sarah, and she bore Tom a son,

16

And also named him Thomas, and he went to Middleton,
Thomas married Mary Ellen, in 1854,
On all fool's day believe me, need I tell you anymore,
They had a son called Thomas, but his relatives were few,
As his only sister died, when she was only twenty-two,
Thomas, he got married, in 1881,
To Harriet who gave birth, to a baby bouncing son,
And he too was a Thomas, complete with postman's sack,
He lived in Sutton Coldfield, and he was known as Jack
Now Jack, he was my granddad, and he knew Fishers Mill,
And that completes the story, regarding Jack and Jill,
Except my six greats grandfather, and Jill's I'll have you know,
Was in fact the same man born so many years ago,
Mothers, fathers, sisters, brothers, sons here in their dozens,
Now Mrs Sidaway and I, are really seventh cousins!

Verily 1st Earl of Runnymede

Fare thee well to an old Hero...............

(An Ex-Marine and work colleague of the author called Woody, a highly efficient and disciplined Prison Officer, was chastised for a minor infringement of the required professional code of conduct)

I used to worship Woody, and thought it all would last,
But Woody now is only just, a legend of the past,
The fact is someone different, has come up on the scene,
Who is even more a hero than an ageing ex-Marine,
Yes, now I worship someone else, and here's the reason why,
Woody never wore his prison issue, clip on tie.

Yes, Woody superhero, he gave a good rendition,
But now has got to make room for some damn good competition,
Admittedly the new boy, was never ex Marines,
But he leads us by example, and at mealtimes eats his greens,
Ex Marines are always on the go, and so perhaps that's why,
Woody never wore his prison issue, clip on tie.

Poor Woody he is ageing, the signs are on the way,
Incontinence and Haemorrhoids, his hair is turning grey,
But although an ageing hero, it pays not to forget,
That what you see in Woody, is precisely what you get,
Rumours droop the landings, the new boy uses dye,
But at least he always wears his prison issue, clip on tie.

And so, it's farewell Woody, companion and friend,
Another chapter opens, and one comes to an end,
You were good as superhero, and you played the part for long,

But you never realised that things had started to go wrong,
You see, it's like this Woody, this is something that I've learned,
You've got to be more flexible where heroes are concerned,
To really be a hero, when girls swoon, when you go by,
Make sure you always wear, your prison issue, clip on tie.

Verily 1st earl of Runnymede

Mum and Dad

It was great to be young, though I'm now out of touch,
of those days with so little, for we hadn't that much,
It's a fact, it is true, we were too scared to speak,
only one pair of shoes, only one bath a week,
We had table and chairs, and a sofa two-seater,
there was no central heating, just a paraffin heater,
Plus, a fire which burned coal, and we'd take it in turn
, throwing on other things, we could find that would burn,
Of damp there was none, and we didn't have mould,
so, it's true that we never, complained of the cold,
And although not a palace, room enough it could give,
so, for us was a fair, and a nice place to live,
Mum made porridge for breakfast, but sometimes a fry,
she would bake her own cakes, treacle tart, apple pie,
On Sundays we always, for breakfast had least,
but for dinner we always indulged in a feast,
Roasted beef, pork or lamb, and potatoes of course,
either with Yorkshire pud or mum's homemade mint sauce,
And when eating her puddings, you'd have to be quick,
lest a chunk would go missing, from your Spotted Dick,
And that could've cost you a paper wrapped tanner,
yes, we ate just as well, as the Lord of the Manor,
We had our own chickens, each had their own name,
someone let them escape, of course I got the blame,
Yes, we chased all them chickens, until we got thinner,
but felt awful guilty, when we ate one for dinner,
There was Grandma in Sutton, living right by the park,
where we'd play all day long, then come home in the dark,
She would talk of past family, and regards what she'd said,
how I wish I had listened, more closely instead,
Gran's house it was large, a warren of doors,

behind each was excitement, spread over three floors,
Being up in the attic, we could not get enough,
an Aladdin's Cave full, of abandoned old stuff,
And the cellar came next, ghostly dark, musty smell,
for us kids a brick stairwell and the gateway to hell,
Our neighbour, the portly, Mrs Caldwell went wild,
I am told lost her biscuits, to an unruly child,
Fingers pointing at me, tell-tale crumbs on a plate,
it was deemed I was guilty, as I'd put on some weight,
And the Tale of the Tadpoles, being buried alive,
not a criminal act, I was only aged five,
Dad had gooseberry bushes, and rhubarb of course,
both sustained by the droppings, of the milkman's old horse,
And being the youngest, I was always the one,
who was sent to retrieve, what the old horse had done,
Fairly touching I'd say, notwithstanding the wit,
for it's true my first job, it was shovelling … horse muck!
Dustmen emptying bins, postmen came by and went,
and the man with a hat, always called for the rent,
I remember the radio, the archers and stuff,
of the radio soaps, mum could not get enough,
Whereas dad he would listen, while eating his toast,
to the forecast for shipping, around Britain's long coast,
Which again is quite strange, and worth adding a note,
for dad travelled to work, on a bus not a boat,
He left early for work and he came home quite late
, I can still hear the sound of him shutting the gate,
Then our faces would bear a quite discerning grin,
wonderin' what sort of mood he was coming home in,
Was he happy enough, or at work come to grief,
when he acted quite normal, it was such a relief,
But if troubled or crass, angry, cross or was vexed,
we kids never knew, if or what to expect,
For in front of each other we'd have to lose face,
on the pretext perhaps, of some shoes out of place,

21

And that haunting it robbed us, of so many things,
like the confident child, that good parenting brings,
I feel sadness at times, even that's hard to say,
for I truly wish things had not turned out that way,
But in those days the men, having physical strength,
kept their women and children, away at arm's length,
Woe betide any housewife, was the unwritten law,
who did not serve his dinner, as he walked through the door,
Though in time old dad waned, his own ego grew small,
and he learned that equality was deserved by us all,
But he struggled adjusting to the world whizzing by,
and instead thought it best, to let sleeping dogs lie,
And contented himself, looking after the chum,
who had loved him the most, and of course that was mum,
She was born with no spite, of regrets none to say,
she was loyal to all, but she then passed away,
Whereas Dad knowing well that his days would not last,
he was haunted by things he had done in the past,
He spoke much of his prospects, of our mum in the main,
of his hopes that he may, meet up with her again,
Yes, I witnessed his suffering, his good life it waned,
an uncomfortable end, though he never complained,
So endeth a chapter, both parents were gone,
but it's true what they say, life it has to go on,
Looking back, I can see, both were victims I felt,
and lived out the life, with the cards they'd been dealt,
As for me I am grateful, like never before,
and I'd give my right arm, to embrace them once more.

Verily 1st Earl of Runnymede

A Week in Verse

(A typical week for the average married couple)

Sunday is the Lord's day, in church and chapel where,
People go and give their thanks, in song as well as prayer,
Monday is the worst day, no special treat or perk,
It's when the population, has to clock on back to work,
Tuesday's are for sticky buns, for cakes and other stuff,
And most of all God's children, simply cannot get enough,
Wednesday is the bath night, until you're in your teens,
A time for getting out the soap, toy boats and submarines,
Thursdays can be boring, and lacking basic thrills,
A time to go out shopping, mowing lawns and paying bills,
Fridays can be tasty, a time to lick your lips,
Two rounds of bread and butter with a battered fish and chips,
But Saturday's the best night, for him it's celebrating,
But only if he promises . . .... to do some decorating

Verily 1st Earl of Runnymede

Poyntzpass

(It was discovered that the author's brother and sister-in-Law parked up late one
Saturday evening by a lonely farm gate in Poyntzpass and were overcome by passion)

Some people go ice skating, on the local lake or rink,
Some stay at home and watch TV, while others take a drink,
But if you want excitement, say an evening full of class,
Just pick a date, and a farmer's gate, down the back roads of
Poyntzpass!

The pictures can be pleasant, the experience is real,
And dining out has its rewards, a very tasty meal,
Both are quite expensive, and cost a lot of brass,
But can't compete, with a car's back seat, down the back roads of
Poyntzpass!

Now me I like my climbing, I find it's hard to beat,
Standing on a mountain top, at several thousand feet,
But I'd come down in a hurry, Even slide down on my ass,
If I had a date, by a farmer's gate, down the back roads of Poyntzpass!

So, if you're travelling to Scarva, starting off from Tandragee,
It's late on Saturday evening, and you're feeling fancy free,
Don't be stopping on the tarmac, or parking on the grass,
Just find a date, and a farmer's gate, down the back roads of
Poyntzpass!

Verily 1st Earl of Runnymede

It's Snowing!

Does it snow in heaven? I'd like to think it does,
Angels could build a snowman and make stars just like us
Lovely little snowflakes, upon a button moon.
When will we see the snow again, it could be very soon?
Its lovely seeing snowflakes they glisten as they fall
You can even roll the snow up and make a great big ball.
Snowball fights and snowmen, kiddies on their sledge.
Come in and get warm now, it's nearly time for bed.

Dora Blandford

Ben Nevis

(The author climbed Scotland's highest mountain and left this on the summit)

This Gaelic piece of granite,
Amid the Scottish Highlands,
Is the tallest and the grandest,
In all the British Islands,
Ben Nevis is to Scotsmen,
A symbol if you like,
The equivalent in my country
Is the mountain Scafell Pike,
Therefore, I do admit,
Although I feel no real disgrace,
That England's premier mountain,
Must take second place,
But in conquering Ben Nevis,
Out of breath and with a thirst,
You can bet your bowl of porridge,
That the English climbed it first!

Verily 1st Earl of Runnymede

Torpedoes

(The author sends some sweets to his friend in the Lake District)

I wandered lonely as a cloud,
That floats on high o'er vale and hill,
Then all at once a host I saw,
And thought, I'll give my friend a thrill,
Ten thousand saw I at a glance,
There in a bottle, at the top,
And thus, I parted with some cash,
There at Stone's famous, sweetie shop,
You need not guess, I'm sure you know,
Your favourite sweets, could think to send,
Torpedoes, half a pound methinks,
For you, a very special friend!

Verily 1st Earl of Runnymede

This is your Life

(The author's take on that program for a friend's 60th birthday)

With evidence gathered, and hearsay that lends, from both your good
children, your family and friends,
and sworn affitt-David from Sherry your wife, Tonight Mr Rory Clay,
this is your life.
Born during the war, in the year nineteen forty, when the country was
blacked out, some couples were naughty,
and embarrassingly so, it is true more than maybe, that it's all thanks to
Hitler, for Mrs Clay's baby!

His christening took place with his naming in ink, Anthony, Rory, and
one other, I think.
It's been kept in a locker, well under his hat, Auspicious, Aubretia, it's
something like that,
Now your secrets with me, and there it will stay, lest it cause you a red
face, on this special day,
I understand well, and indeed it is true, that if I were named Aubrey, I'd
hang myself too!

Then Rory signed up, for a stint in the forces, And after his training
and several courses,
Passed out at St Vincent, a brand-new A.B, then with snorkel and
paddle, he headed for sea,
In HMS Pembroke, Victorious, and Blake, He sailed round the globe,
with a girl in each wake,
But then he met Sherry, and later he thanked her, for stealing his heart,
and weighing his anchor!
Now Sherry would pack, Rory's case without thought, A job that she
did, when he went back to port,
She once occurred error, which made naval news, And packed winkle
pickers, instead of his shoes,

28

There was nothing to do, the mistake had been made, and so Rory
wore them, to go on parade,
It could have been worse, just think of the mocking's, If Sherry had
packed him, suspender and stockings!

Now Rory was a radar man, a huff duff chuff was he, Electronics was
his forte, and his speciality,
A man au fait with physics, a man who never panics, someone who
could lecture, on Quantum, Mechanics,
But sadly, it was noticed, at a party by a few, That with the age of
mobile phones, he's met his Waterloo,
He tried to make a local call, and is not connected yet, He was dialling
on the remote control, of Sharon's TV set!

And so, it's with sincerity, that all of us we send, Greetings to you Rory,
the father, husband, friend,
Paying tribute to those sixty years, comparing you to saints, we wanted
you to know, that we all have no complaints,
If husbands came to order, fathers made to measure, if friends were
picked according to, how much they gave in pleasure,
Dear Rory, please be reassured, and all of this is true, for all these
worldly choices, we would've still picked you!

Verily 1st Earl of Runnymede

Message in a Bottle

(The author's sister, having won a fine bottle of single malt in a raffle, was petitioned by her son Richard for its contents, but she declined to be so generous. Declaring that it was to be kept for a special occasion, the seal was finally broken, and the contents put to good use when the author became a trifle miffed after getting his car bogged down in mud and was compelled to summon costly assistance. The threat of retribution followed, his nephew, in a letter addressed to "A very old Uncle" inferred that the author had consumed the contents of his rightful inheritance. The gauntlet had been thrown to the floor - and retrieved with the author's words below.)

With respect to the question, in the letter I got, if asked whether guilty,
I'd say I was not,
There was circumstance plenty, on this sad occasion, which I purport
rightly, is my mitigation,
You see on the night, my car came to pass, and ventured misfortune, a
hole in the grass,
I was frustrate and angry, and livid no less, in the medical term, I was
suffering from stress!

With the health service striving and straining to cope, no medicines
handy, I then lost all hope,
Till your mum found a way to relieve my frustration, and said it was
good to restore circulation,
If I had a Wee Dram or another indeed, and so to oblige, of course I
agreed,
The whisky was smooth although it was cold, it was probably say about
12 years old.!

From that moment on, I discarded my coat, for I warmed up quite
nicely, as it slid down my throat,
The second drink vanished, so the third one I waited, but it too got
lost, or evaporated,

30

The fourth, fifth and sixth one, it was so hard to tell, like the seventh
one poured, they all went down well,
The eighth and the ninth and the tenth one as such, to be truthful I
cannot, remember that much.!

Now my sister has said, though I took it in fun, that she had been asked
by the likes of her son,
He'd petitioned a favour, and begged during talk, for a sniff of the
bottle, or a lick of the cork,
But her answer was curt, she said if you like, you can put on your clips,
and get on your bike,
This bottle here stays, for reason another, the fact is I have me, a very
fine Brother.!

Now I know to be truthful, it's hard to accept, that I drank most the
contents, of what your mum kept,
I know what you're thinking, you're down in a ditch, and wondering
why life, is a hell of a bitch,
But it pays to remember, the better the soon, old instruments can, play
a very sweet tune,
So, you see master Richard, irrespective of thirst,
T'was me your old uncle, who got in there first.!

Verily 1st Earl of Runnymede

A Thanks

(The author receives a thank you card and reciprocates)

Having finished my round, I came home, and I found,
That the postman had called, I could see,
For beside the front door, was a card on the floor,
And the name on the card, it was me,
Now I wondered who'd bought, a nice card but I thought,
Though it got me excited it's true,
Such a treat for my eyes, what a lovely surprise,
When I saw that the card was from you,
Now the words were so nice, that I've read it now twice,
For it says "Thanks for my thoughtfulness"
Sending me all or most, of a thanks in the post,
Yes, your gesture has served to impress,
Reading that here in Stone, has brought thoughts of my own,
And the main one that now springs to mind,
Is how much thanks are due, not to me, but to you,
For you're also so thoughtful and kind.

Verily 1st Earl of Runnymede

Valentine Request

(An endearment by the author but not to be taken too seriously)

My darling sweet girl, pray no wonder I watch,
With a tear in my eye while you're drinking my scotch,
And as most of its gone, please don't think I'm a whinger,
But it would have been nice if you'd left some dry ginger,
The lemonade's finished, of wine I'm bereft,
And that Brandy I bought, well there's so little left,
My fridge has no food, there is just nothing there,
My larder and cupboards, are empty and bare,
In the past I had mice eating bits off the floor,
But now they've moved out, and are living next door,
And yet as I write, with no crumb for my plate,
It would seem that in contrast, you're putting on weight,
Now it's true that you're not, just my girlfriend by chance,
We've walked up some hills and have partnered in dance,
Now you've drunk all my brandy, scotch, ginger and wine,
Why not finish it off and be my Valentine?

Verily 1st Earl of Runnymede

Hedgehogs

Hedgehogs roam around at night,
If you're lucky, you may catch sight.
Spikey and prickly, with a black shiny nose,
they can roll up in a ball you know!
Sniffing and snorting, foraging for food,
they keep the slugs down, so that is good.
The numbers are falling, it's so sad to hear,
my heart feels so heavy and I shed a tear.
So long live the hedgehog and keep them right here!
Let's all help them live and thrive with no fear.

Our Hedgehogs

We love to watch our hedgehogs when they come out at night,
One, two or maybe more, it's such an amazing sight.
Sniffing and grunting as they go on their way,
you shouldn't really see them out in the day.
Hedgehogs are really hard to understand,
They're funny little prickly things when they're in your hand.
If you want to help them go along their way,
Make A hole in your fence is what I would say!
Hedgehogs are in decline you know,
They're getting less and less.
So, put some food and water out,
To help them with their stress.

Dora Blandford

Dear Friend

(The author writes sarcastically to a friend)

Looking somewhat forlorn, I was up with the dawn,
and just finished my first cup of tea,
Hearing constant loud snores, from above me because,
my son Tom is still sleeping you see,
As you know I arise, after rubbing my eyes,
at the same time as those on the wing,
Yes, was up with the birds, and now playing with words,
which I don't think is too bad a thing.

Mindful of and mind you, I know someone it's true,
who needs tea to wake up, in a cup,
Who blinks at first sight, at the first ray of light,
that they see when their eyelids go up,
Someone who likes to keep, the same pattern of sleep,
but instead of a kip day to day,
If I'm not overstating, would prefer hibernating,
from early November till May.

I'm not out to impress and I'm sure you will guess,
I am joking as I always do,
And not wishing at all, to disturb with a call,
So instead thought that I'd write to you,
Pray a short little note, an endearment I wrote,
an affectionate mention to make,
In so far and as much, I like keeping in touch,
that's providing of course, you're awake!

Verily 1st Earl of Runnymede

35

Dearest Sister

(The author keeps his sister up to date with the home news)

My apologies first, for the absence of rhyme,
but the truth is I've not, had a great deal of time,
I've been off so long, I'm sluggish and dusty,
my brain is in neutral, my pen has gone rusty,
But I'm due back to work, so I'll have to stay sober,
for I'm due to return, at the end of October,
A prospect hard done, but is easier said,
just the thought has me trembling, and fills me with dread,
So, I' tried to get fit, on something I like,
and decided to go for ten miles on my bike,
The spirit was willing, but my flesh had cross wires,
for I hadn't the strength, to blow up the tyres!

Back the push-bike in mothballs, and now growing roots,
I got out my wet suit, and put on my boots,
Cader Idris was tempting, a challenge was that,
I could take off some inches, of limp ugly fat,
I could go climbing Friday, and calories burn,
and be so much fitter, upon my return,
So, I called little Tom, and suggested we spent,
a pleasant day climbing, and made an ascent,
Tom carried the rucksack, all the way without stop,
then we ate all the contents, while sitting on top,
But I carried it down, I'm an honourable blighter,
but then it was empty, and a good deal more lighter!

We returned home to Stone, I looked like a tramp,
muscles all aching, and suffering from cramp,
My stomach distended, it looked like a bin,
I was so out of breath, that I couldn't suck in,
My ankles were swollen, I had a sore head,
my bones were all creaking, my face had gone red,
I swallowed some "Crampex" and five tubs of salt,
and frequently had, to pull in for a halt,
Whereas someone much younger, pretty fit and in touch,
had found it so easy, and not suffered much,
Tom was prancing about, like a lamb that was frolicking,
and so, I decided, to give him a telling off!

The tomatoes are ripe, the best they have been,
and now are quite red, instead of just green,
My plants are quite healthy, and have been since June,
and most are still boasting, a colourful bloom,
I moved some around, after which they looked fine,
all part of my bachelor, image design,
And I hoped that Diana, would greatly approve,
of several plants, being put on the move,
Yes, it troubled me much, a thought was just striking,
and I hoped that the moves, were all to her liking,
So, taking precaution, in case I'm not right,
I dug up the plants, and I moved them at night!

Your invite for dinner, next Sunday sounds fair,
and believe me dear sister, I'm sure to be there,
I'll not miss the chance, of a roast from the spit,
and promise that I, will eat every bit,
Christo and Ness, are as keen as can be,
both have good appetite's, quite similar to me,
They will be there, and hope it is fine,
if they bring you a couple, of bottles of wine,
I've asked Tom and Sally, pray regards they both send,
and both have said yes, they would like to attend,

No doubt Sally to help, lay the table and wait,
while Tom has some seconds, and then licks his plate!

Now that's all from the "George's" of Stone for a while,
I hope that the reading, has nurtured a smile,
I'm still feeling stiff, but I'm hopeful I'll foil,
my pains now I'm taking, some Cod Liver Oil,
I'll be down this week, maybe Thursday who knows,
what with the wedding, I've got to buy clothes,
I tried on my grey suit, it just wouldn't button,
I was dressed like a young lamb, and looking like mutton,
The trousers they fitted, but I had to force it,
they felt like a Michelin, vulcanised corset,
So, I went to the tailors, but I couldn't help curse,
when they asked me to call, for an estimate first!

Verily 1st Earl of Runnymede

Dinner Invitation

(The author invites his sister for dinner)

My thanks for the text, which you sent me today,
It was nice but believe me, there's things I must say,
Although not for the first time, your message gave rise,
To my eyebrows indeed, for it was a surprise,
My morning's gone well, the hours well taken,
I had cereal which, was then followed by bacon,
Plus, a hot cup of tea, no it wasn't my first,
I brewed several more, as you know I have thirst,
Then I have cancelled my contract, with BT the phone,
For I don't use the landline when I am in Stone,
I've forwarded letters, a task far from hard,
And settled in full what I owe Barclaycard
Then I cleaned up my amp, now it looks in good stead,
Folded my clothes and I've just made the bed,
I've vacuumed and polished, and dusted throughout,
Sorted my papers and thrown rubbish out,
I then had some thoughts, which came into bloom,
And organised changes, in my hobby Room,
There to straighten the pictures, and brush the mouse mat,
Tidy the drawers, and move this and that,
Then put things away, leaving nothing amiss,
Then with much sharpened wits, sat to write all of this,
Well that was my morning, not much of a perk,
And shortly will I, be off going to work,
But was wondering if, as you're such a good friend,
In the next week or two, and are at a loose end,
If you'd care to meet up, to be dined like a queen,
And share in a sample of Stafford cuisine,
For a Toby Jug Carvery, with gravy and all,
And if that sounds nice sis, just give us a call.

Verily 1st Earl of Runnymede

Oooooooh Aaaaaaah

(The author is contacted by an old army friend residing in Cornwall)

Was it wishes come true, I talking to you,
Though your accent it threw me at first,
For it sounded as if maybe you had a cold,
Or perhaps you were choking with thirst,
Now I don't understand, having travelled the land,
You would think I could place every county,
But your voice although shy, sounded like Captain Bligh,
Or the first mate of HMS Bounty.

Now there's no need to fret, or be getting upset,
For you know that when all's said and done,
I've a GCSE, in raw humour you see,
And a masters at just poking fun,
Plus, I tell a few jokes, when at work to the blokes,
And occasionally to all the staff,
For they think it's a perk, when we're all in at work,
And besides it costs nothing to laugh.

I do housework today, keeping cobwebs at bay,
Change the bedding and sheets as you do,
Then I tidy the place, lest it all fall from grace,
And do all of the ironing too,
Push a vacuum around, till no dust can be found,
Pray I'm not paid so much as a guinea,
Then the last thing of all, I go into the hall,
And finally hang up my Pinney.

But it's not hung up yet, I've the shopping to get,
And other chores too don't you know,
Like there's more than one ledge, needs a good spray of Pledge,
With a "J cloth" that's raring to go,
So, I better get back on the treadmill again,
But before I sign off with adieu,
If anyone says on the phone now OooooH AaaaaH,
At least I will know that it's you.

Verily 1st Earl of Runnymede

Dearest Sally

(Guess who the author's girlfriend is)

As it's Valentine's day, a thought came my way,
About all the things we have done,
Notwithstanding my wit, you have to admit,
It all has been jolly good fun,
We've seen almond trees, tried to speak Portuguese,
And we gave "Par-lay-vou-ing" a chance,
Calling on Finistere, stunning beaches were there,
When we visited Nessy in France,
There was walking by Jove, down at Mullion Cove,
On the coastal path, very nice too,
You went out for a hike, on the back of John's bike,
But you hung on, as all ladies do,
Other ventures of course, like you riding that horse,
Which stopped down the lane for a "wee"
When we felt like a munch, Cornish pasties for lunch,
And you shooting my gun out to sea,
Climbed a mountain in Wales, walked the Windermere dales,
And taken short walks, now and then,
Rode our bikes wearing smiles, for nigh thirteen miles,
And seen Blackpool, with Mervyn and Gwen,
Two funerals that had, overtones very sad,
And been to more than one wedding,
Taken you, out to choose, forty-four, pairs of shoes,
And visited Tom down in Reading,
And that's how it been, you and me, rather keen,
Building snowmen in cold frosty weather,
Or playing in sand, on the beach hand in hand,
Sharing much of our free time together,
As for me, was well spent, yes I'm more than content,

And no more, could a happy boy be,
You're my own "Little Star" and I like what you are,
That's why you're so special to me,
So, I just want to say, on this romantic day,
All the pleasures will surely be mine,
If you give me a kiss, after reading all this,
And say . . . . . . you'll be my Valentine!

Verily 1st Earl of Runnymede

The Pretty Girl

(The author's girlfriend has a new modern hair style)

I walked without, so much a care,
To meet a special girl did I
In Stone, along the high street there,
And saw a sight, that pleased my eye,
No more a cosy on a rock,
And missing were the twists and curl,
I looked and thought how glad I am,
To have me, such a pretty girl.

Verily 1st Earl of Runnymede

(The Author had a flare up of her knee)

My blooming painful knee

My blooming painful knee has flared up once again.
I twisted it the other day and ouch it gave me pain.
I hobbled to the doctor and told him how it felt,
He said to use an ice pack leave on until it melts.
He also gave me gel and pills to ease the pain you know,
And even sent me down the road to have some physio.
The pain it wasn't going it's with me all day long,
I'm waiting for injections down in SA one.
I'm glad to say with much relief that steroid jab did good,
The inflammations going down like it blooming should.
Hydrotherapy pool were trying, the weightless exercise,
And hopefully get better before my very eyes.

Dora Blandford

Mrs Sally Wingepot

(Let's just say not the best week)

This is Mrs Wingepot, if you want to take a peek,
And hasn't had the best of luck, from Thursday of last week,
She caught a cold last Friday, which caused her nose to bloat,
But worst of all on Saturday, she had a poorly throat,
She saw her mum on Sunday, her son he gave off sparks,
The pair of them were so unkind, with comments and remarks,
On Monday she was snoffling, then found she couldn't hear,
Apart from coming out her nose, the cold got in her ear,
Come Tuesday she went shopping, but sadly wasn't wise,
Saw a lovely trendy skirt, but got a different size,
On Friday she was clocking off, she finished rather late,
And had a punch up with a girl, a trifle overweight,
But now the week was over, well for now at any rate,
And so, she chewed a toffee, let's say to celebrate,
But was only just a minute, when I heard a sorry shout,
The toffee although very nice, had pulled a filling out,
But worst of all for me at least, it's ruined my tonight,
As she now can't put on lip-gloss, 'till the dentist puts it right!

Verily 1st Earl of Runnymede

My Prize Possession

(Not to be confused with a famous savoury spread, this little pot is the author's pet name for his girlfriend)

I live a short way out of town,
Beside the river Trent,
I've not amassed a fortune,
But what I've earned is not all spent,
I've got CDs and two TVs,
A mobile phone and car,
A wardrobe bursting at the seams,
A camera and guitar,
Yes I've lots of prize possessions,
And I'm not one to boast,
But my "Little Pot o' Veggie-Mite"
Is the one I love the most.

Verily 1st Earl of Runnymede

Sex for Her

(The author's take on the subject and sent to a friend on her 65th Birthday)

At the young age of five, a girl can't help guess,
Why a boy is in trousers, and she's in a dress,
At fifteen she reads, about boys in a book,
What they keep in their trousers, and just wants a look,
At twenty-five well, by then she's quite wise,
And with all of her friends, all she talks of is size,
At thirty-five well, having passion to burn,
Being frank it's by then, that she's no more to learn,
At forty-five that's, when she can't get enough,
So, she wears black suspenders, nice perfume and stuff,
At fifty-five sex, is the same old refrain,
A night in the sheets, is just down memory lane,
But at sixty-five that's, when her nights are the best,
With a real comfy pillow, and a decent night's rest.

Verily 1st Earl of Runnymede

The Victoria Sponge

(A dear friend sent the author and his wife a cake, but it arrived at the same time as their son)

We were sitting at home, we were down, we were miffed,
When my father arrived, he was bearing a gift,
Was it chocolate or sweeties, booty or swag,
We just couldn't wait, so we looked in the bag,
And there to be seen was a lovely surprise,
A cake upon which, we could both feast our eye's,
We took off the wrapper, it looked really nice,
And both helped ourselves to a very big slice,
The sponge was delicious, so fluffy and light,
The filling was creamy, you'd made it just right,
Then we found a large tin, and put it away,
With aims to indulge, the very next day,
Now life's very sweet from the day you are born,
But it's true with each rose, there is always a thorn,
And in our case the cake, was a means to an end,
But arrived when our son, came home that weekend,
And the youngsters of late, have good cause to smile,
They can sniff out a good cake, at over a mile,
And despite our precautions, of hiding the tin,
Tom's sticky fingers, they found a way in,
So, if there's a sequel, and in wisdom decree,
To bake yet another, for Diana and me,
Would you do us a favour, and grant us a perk,
Send it to us, when our Tom's back at work!

Verily 1st Earl of Runnymede

49

Corran Tuathail

(The author climbed Ireland's highest Mountain and left a copy of this on the summit)

Standing up here on the summit, I cannot help thinking how small,
Are the problems of living in harmony, if there is a problem at all,
For I'm told that the English and Irish, blame each other for all that is
wrong,
Five hundred years, of blood sweat and tears, is the reason they don't
get along,
But myself I consider it foolish, and as always, I speak as I find,
I have always regarded all Irish folk, as generous, helpful and kind.

It's said that the Irish remember, and in England we also abide,
We remember the likes of young private Quigg, at a time when we
fought side by side,
A young volunteer who in 1915, seven times he crawled out to the wire,
To rescue a wounded young soldier, and six more, which he did under
fire,
If I had to describe, this brave Irish lad, for words, I would be at a loss,
And he was just one, who took on the Hun, and won the Victoria
Cross.

Now the Irish must like us a bit for apart, from the help that they gave
in the wars,
Many a million of Irish descent, are settled upon English shores,
And they welcome us into their Shamrock clubs, after work at the end
of the day,
To sample a drink on a bar stool, where the Guinness flows only one
way,
And we Saxons, we think that we're drinkers, and also, we like to
compete,
But we never would challenge the Micks to a duel, for we know it
would end in defeat.

I have really enjoyed my short holiday, I'll be coming to Ireland again,
But there's just a couple of niggling things, about which I'm compelled
to complain,
There was no pot of gold at the rainbow's end, there were no
leprechauns, and what's more,
I found lots of good Irish clover, but all had three leaves, and not four,
And as for the forty odd greens to be seen, indeed every shade it was
fine,
Except I couldn't see forty, I could only make out Thirty-Nine.

Verily 1st Earl of Runnymede

Getting Young Sarah to Ring

(The author was expecting a call from his friend's daughter)

With the Christmas all done, having had, lots of fun,
I was saddened I have to admit,
I expected a call, but received none at all,
Pray I missed your good humour, and wit,
I just couldn't wait, so I called Santa late,
And in lieu of the presents he'd bring,
Listen Santa I said, I would settle instead,
If you'd just get young Sarah to ring,
Listen Gerry said he, how can I guarantee,
She's ambitious with boys don't you know,
For she's out to seduce, every boy on the loose,
And she's still the Royal Navy to go,
Half the Kings London Horse, most the Royal Air Force,
The second Battalion, the Queens,
Five cadets, training done, from the camp Bovington,
And the odd one or two young Marines,
Irish Guards two platoons, the Hussars and Dragoons,
And some Grenadiers in ceremonial dress,
Forty Para's or more, the entire Camel Corps,
Plus, the Gurkhas and eight SAS,
Santa said to me twice, why not take my advice,
With all these boys waiting, it's bleak,
It will take her a while, so just sit back and smile,
And try ringing her back in a week!

Verily 1st Earl of Runnymede

A Sixtieth Birthday

(The author commemorates a friend's 60th birthday)

What can we say as the proud moment nears?
To a friend who's been with us for nigh sixty years,
A trained Paramedic, on the front line each day,
Who cared for his patients in every way,
And who better to comfort, the sick and the sadder,
Those who've broken a leg, or have fell from a ladder,
Though if any got stroppy, or cheeky by 'eck,
They'd soon have a tourniquet, wrapped round their neck.

Now Ken he goes swimming, that's what I call cool,
And often you'll see him, there down at the pool,
I suppose it's release, from work induced tension,
After all it's a hard way of one earning one's pension,
But he goes quite a lot, and his friends, well they speak,
Of concerns as he goes, maybe three times a week,
Making splashes is better, than giving out pills,
But his ears now have gone, and instead he's grown Gills.

As for me regards dealings, with Ken I've had loads,
In the form of a wedding, which took place in Rhodes,
He wanted a beach towel, which is all very nice,
So, we went shop to shop, to locate the best price,
Ken bartered in pennies, but he wasn't impressed,
As for me what I wanted, was to stop for a rest,
After long hours of haggling, from noon 'till half three,
I gave Ken a fiver and said Have one on me.

Now regards the above, I know you'll have guessed,
The verses were thought of, and written in jest,
And are sent with best wishes, from me to a friend,
For your sixtieth birthday, this coming weekend,
As for offering wisdom, not that I'm an owl,
Methinks now's the time, if you're wanting that towel,
Rhodes is wracked with inflation, so take my advice,
Nip over and get one, they're now half the price.

Verily 1st Earl of Runnymede

Mum I miss you still

Mum I came home you were gone! Was told you had passed away.
I was young just twelve, I didn't know what to say.
In silence my pain, my hurt, an emptiness inside me grew,
Were you coming back I thought, but something inside me knew.
No! You were gone, gone forever, I wouldn't see you again.
No time to mourn or grieve, no one to console my pain.
I'm older now and nothing much has changed.
You're in my heart, you're in my soul, you're in my brain.
Mum I miss you still, it hurts my heart so much.
I want a kiss, a cuddle, and feel a mother's touch.
I look around and see the bond, with daughters and their mum.
I'm jealous, I'm angry, I'm empty! I didn't get to have one.
I'm still grieving for you inside; it really makes me ill.
Mum I miss you; I miss you still.

Dora Blandford

Mates Forever

(The author, due to go on a date that evening, is presented with a very personal gift from a friend)

Hello, Said Tony, hi said I, you're looking darned exquisite,
And Tony said "I always do, when paying you a visit"
He said he'd been out shopping, and much to his delight,
Saw something in the chemist shop, I might need Wednesday night,
And as I'd been a special friend, and he had surplus coins,
He'd bought for me a little gift, to help me oil my loins!

Excitement gripped me by the lip, I couldn't wait to look,
Was it pheromonal aftershave, or just a dirty book,
A vacuum pump expander, or revitalising milk,
Strawberry flavour lubricant, or underpants of silk,
I could see the packet legend, which said "Before you go on dates"
Don't forget your KY Jelly, and make sure you've got your mates!

Now these Condoms Tony bought me, they came complete with tread,
He hadn't bought me Gossamers, but Michelins instead,
With proven ZX pattern, for a far more sensual trip,
Which guaranteed whilst cornering, to give you extra grip,
And fair play yes I need it, for I'm hung just like a barge,
But why did Tony buy me small, when I need the Extra-Large!

And so, it is with gratitude, I had to write and say,
A very hearty thank you, for your gift received today,
As you know it's been a while, since my appetite's been wet,
I need all the encouragement, and help that I can get,
So, to make sure I perform real well, and carry out my functions,
Perhaps you'd care to tell me, what you did with the instructions!

Verily 1st Earl of Runnymede

Dear Neighbour

(A neighbour received this from the author after suffering a noisy weekend
and a bright one too, as the same neighbour had installed a huge flood light)

I hope this my poem will give no offence,
It's regards last weekend, besides other events,
I'd been washing the clothes, 'tis my duty, a must,
But when hung out to dry, they got covered in dust,
So, I rinsed them once more, and with weather so fine,
I ventured with pegs, to refill the line,
But on checking them later I experienced dismay,
For my garden resembled, the city Pompeii,
Though it wasn't hot ash, which fell from the blue,
I couldn't be sure, but I had me a clue,
You see all the weekend, far as I could tell,
Including Bank holiday Monday as well,
All peace was forsaken and from that moment on,
The silence was shattered, and quiet long gone,
For in place of the sounds, of songbirds so keen,
Was the whine of a motorised cutting machine,
I wouldn't complain but it hurt, all those jeers,
From all those who saw me with wool in my ears,
If you doubt what I write, then pray ask Meg and Jeff,
when the cutting abated, I thought I'd gone deaf,
I tell you no lies, and these are the facts,
My ears now get cramp, from the excess of wax,
But there's more to this story to come even still,
So, don't put this down, and read on if you will,
Was today in late evening, my stomach to please,
I made a thick sandwich, containing some cheese,
And ventured the garden, to eat in the night,
But was caught unawares, by a bright shining light,
My night vision gone, if not certainly most,
My bread in no time had been turned into toast,
The garden's been ruined, the place is a wreck,
My sunflower looked round, and twisted it's neck,
The birds all awoke, and ruffled their plume,
Plants lifted their heads, and then came into bloom,

Now it's been a long story but again a long week,
Composed in good faith, and I'd say tongue in cheek,
Though there is a small favour I'm leaving to chance,
Next time for a warning, and well in advance,
A couple of days is now is all that I ask,
Just so I can put on, my helmet and mask.

Verily 1st Earl of Runnymede

Member of Staff of the Week 3

(The author overheard a work colleague called Tom telling others of his previous career in the RAF, how apparently there was nothing and nowhere he hadn't been, seen, done or flew, then it was found that he only drove a bus)

I was sitting in the workplace, and someone said Hey Jed,
I asked Tom was he in the RAF, and this is what Tom said...

I've flown Chinooks out of Changi, from Benson Buccaneers,
Flown Wellingtons from Wycombe and was doing it for years,
Flown Sorties from Seleetar, it gave me such a thrill,
And piloted a Spitfire from the likes of Biggin Hill,
I've flown in sunny weather, I've flown in bad conditions,
And I never missed the target when I went on bombing missions,
I've taken off from runways, I've taken off from Carriers,
I cleared the skies of Argies, when I was flying Harriers,
I've looped the loop in Lightnings, and flown them in the wet,
Was in the Red Arrows more than once and flew a Phantom Jet,
Yes, I was in the R.A.F the best of all careers,
And ended up a Sergeant after two and twenty years,
And I really was admired, by the top brass in the RAF,
Especially all the Generals and Air Force chief of Staff,
You see I made a small request and asked to be transferred,
And my application to the Station office was referred,
I thought I'd been successful, but I couldn't help but frown,
When the C.O said I'm sorry Tom, I've had to turn it down,
I said OK let's have it, why can't you let me go,
Well fair enough I'll tell you said the Aerodrome C.O,
You're just too good a worker, you're dam good looking too,
You are witty and intelligent, and no one else will do,
You're charming at the best of times, you're never coy or shy,
And all the girls would shed a tear, if you should say goodbye,
But the reason why you're staying, and sadly this is true,
No one sweeps the runway Tom, not half as good as you

Verily 1st Earl of Runnymede

A Tribute to Mick

(The author was asked to write a tribute to a deserving work colleague, to be read at his farewell dinner)

After long distinguished service, for more than forty years,
In two difficult environments and challenging careers,
The first as Able Seaman, where his duties I suppose,
Included drinking lots of grog, aboard the Mary Rose,
But after many years at sea, and known as hello sailor,
Mick finally got shore leave, and became a Stafford Gaoler,
There to practice all the many skills, he learnt from HMS,
Like scrounging tea and coffee, from his colleagues in the mess,
Like resolving disagreements, if he found he couldn't win,
Arbitration in his language, was a good kick on the shin,
But he's had his share of hardships, and most were not his fault,
Like the eagle tattoo on his back, that's now begun to moult,
And the time that he went swimming, having thrown off all his clothes,
But was put off by a commentator, shouting Thar she Blows,
But on a note more serious, to a man who's full of vigour,
He's a Captain Birds eye lookalike, and a much-respected figure,
Whose philosophy was simple, the carrot and the whip,
In the Navy and the Prison yes, he ran a tidy ship,
So, in keeping with good practice, be upstanding for a toast,
Let's raise a glass and drink to Mick, and wish for him the most,
After that you men can shake his hand, and all you girls can kiss him,
Cause when he's gone, we all agree, by Christ we're going to Miss him!

Verily 1st Earl of Runnymede

(The Author and her sister know that their brothers are not as strong, as they think they are)

Brothers

Brothers think that they are strong, they keep things locked inside.
Never showing emotion, they seem to want to hide!
We know they must be hurting; we know it must be true.
They have been through lots of things, just like me and you.
Maybe control their feelings? and brush them to the side.
Brothers being brothers like to be our guide.
Men don't show their feelings, it's just a guessing game.
But really deep deep down inside, they're feeling just the same.
Lots have happened over the years, you getting through tough times,
It's made you even more aware, of the time that's passing by.
I'd like to say to my big Bros. don't hold things deep inside,
Let out all of your feelings, just like the rolling tide.
We've been through things together, in early childhood years,
And just because you're older it's OK to shed some tears.

Dora Blandford

The Poorly Ex-Marine

(The author hears one of his friends is in hospital and sent him this to cheer him up)

As you know I have a visitor, each morning if not most,
Normally for coffee, plus a round or two of toast,
We chat about all sorts of things, I let him know my views,
He lets me know the gossip, and the latest prison news,
That's when I heard that things of late, were not as they have been,
In so much you're now a patient, and a poorly Ex-Marine!

He said you'd been in hospital, said the details would come later,
And added that you'd problems, sadly south of your equator,
That you'd undergone some kind of test, as patients often do,
But he didn't know the outcome, the results had not come through,
So, I thought I'd write a verse or two, and keep them squeaky clean,
For I'd never be sarcastic, to a poorly Ex-Marine!

I thought of sending chocolates, all varieties and shapes,
A bag of sugared almonds, or a pound of seedless grapes,
Some vitamins, a bowl of fruit, a box of Shredded Wheat,
Anything to help a friend, to get back on his feet,
I even thought of flowers, but I knew you'd not be keen,
One sends bouquets to a lady, not a poorly Ex-Marine!

So instead I've sent my best regards, and hope as from today,
You have a good recovery, and this without delay,
If there's anything that I could do, irrespective of the task,
You can count on my assistance, all you have to do is ask,
Indeed, I'd like the chance to help a friend back on the scene,
For like all your friends, I wish you weren't. . . a poorly Ex-Marine!

Verily 1st Earl of Runnymede

The pleasure of Nieces

(The author here is thanking his big sister for a very enjoyable dinner in the company
of his nieces)

Well I'm sure you'll have guessed, now I'm up and I'm dressed,
that the first thing I'd do was to write,
To commend your precision, and kindly decision,
and send me a dinner invite,
Pray I have to admit, was a pleasure to sit,
at a table well graced and endowed,
And the food that I got, yes, I ate the whole lot,
though licking plates wasn't allowed.

Now I tried to be good, when it came to the pud,
and I swear this is true on my oath,
Of two choices my friend, wishing not to offend,
I thought wise to eat up them both,
Now I cannot deny, second helpings came by,
and a fourth which I ate bereft,
But it's only a myth, that I ate up a fifth,
as by then there was no puddings left.

Such a lovely day spent, on the last day of lent,
starting with a hot drink from the kettle,
Followed by a good few. in fine company who,
were all in good mood and fine fettle,
There was Julie in style, with her far reaching smile,
and Tamzin who's so supersonic,
Only one thing to say, that to me on the day,
the effect was far more than a tonic.

Well it's now the day after, we had all that laughter,
yet my ears are still ringing no less,
And there's no better riches, than Julie in stitches,
an occasion which serves to impress,
But that was not all, there were toddlers on call,
and thinking of someone I grinned,
For last Sunday I found, there is no sweeter sound,
than hearing young Tamzin break wind.

But that was not all, was then Katie called,
and you know what I think of my nieces,
Here there's no need for tact, for indeed it's a fact,
and you know that I love them to pieces,
Katie limping away, on her crutches that day,
after suffering pains in her hip,
Though no parrot or patch, she looked more of a match,
than a pirate without any ship.

So, my thanks once again, for the happy refrain,
amid company so rich in good cause,
Especially big sis, lest I be in remiss,
I'm referring especially to yours,
Now back home my diet, is all peace and quiet,
but at least since my farewell and parting,
Though my ears aren't the best, they can now have a rest,
from the constant noise of Tamzin coughing?

Verily 1st Earl of Runnymede

The wedding invitation

(The author receives an invitation to Samantha's wedding and a promise from Sarah
the bride's sister to get me fixed up with a local girl)

I was sat at the table, devouring my toast,
browsing over what I, had received in the post,
Christmas cards in great numbers, and not without reason,
it is after all, the good festive season,
But amongst greetings plenty, hard to open and handle,
was a card proudly bearing, a white Roman candle,
Or was it I thought, an ice cream to savour,
a conical sort ninety-nine satin flavour,
But then I looked closer, for what seemed like hours,
how silly of me, 'twas a bouquet of flowers,
And on opening such, full of anticipation,
I received your most welcome and kind invitation.

I read all the detail, and endeavoured to see,
then checked as one does, to see if I was free,
No commitments to date, no engagements to lend,
no blind dates or parties, no feasts to attend,
No sunny excursions with monies to spend,
no cocktails, no cruises, no dirty weekends,
No doctor appointments, no calls to be heeded,
or functions where I am regarded as needed,
In fact, when I checked, on the day Sam gets wed,
in lieu of an entry, it was just blank instead,
Which says much of my life and my social career,
as there isn't an entry, for all of next year.

Oh, and just one small item, for Sarah and co,
she said of loose women, that she's in the know,
And with aims well intentioned, my welfare in mind,
a suitable person, would willingly find,
So please tell her an English or preferably Latin,
scantily dressed, in pink or black satin,
With morals unfettered, who drinks by the score,
so, she won't recall, most the evening before,
Now Sarah's reliable, and knows most the town,
and I'm hoping that she, will not let me down,
So, I'm booking a hotel room, to save me much trouble,
and in case I get lucky, I'm booking a Double.

Verily 1st Earl of Runnymede

Winter

(The author does not like the cold)

These chilly winter months I fare, doth bring us nothing but despair,
Our routine is to suffer cold, as winter comes and then takes hold,
The shortened days, so lacking light, the dark and seemly endless night,
Extra clothing bought from stores, to wear if we must go outdoors,
We strive and try, nigh everything, and then hang on until the spring.

You may have noticed how I planned, a glove to wear upon each hand,
A sign of cold and my good form, a way to keep my donnies warm,
My water bottle is the most, at night to keep me warm as toast,
The gently heat, that lends to please, without it, I am sure to freeze,
Each night I dream the morn will bring, a welcome sign of coming
spring.

No matter of, how much the cost, I'd give all to, escape the frost,
There are no lengths I would not go, in order to escape the snow,
The same regards how much the price, I'd pay to rid us of the ice,
And yet in summer months a lot, I've moaned about it being hot,
Mother nature's point's been driven … Come back sun, all is forgiven.

Verily 1st Earl of Runnymede

66

For the Baby

(The author sent all these plus this verse)

A card to send my wishes,
Plus enclosed a small amount,
For you to start a saving and,
The Baby's bank account,
Some clothes to keep the baby snug,
I hope the colours please,
And with aims to warm the baby's feet,
A pair of small bootees,
But the silver I have given,
For it's said that it may bless,
A new-born child with lots of love,
And untold Happiness!

Verily 1st Earl of Runnymede

Dear Merv and Gwen

(It's a Saturday and, as I have nothing planned, I thought I would write you a letter,
For out-doors it is pale, wet and blowing a gale, and the forecast, quite frankly's, no better,
So, I sharpened my wit, found a good place to sit, and considered that I could do worse,
If I listed our views, gossip, comments and news, and scribbled them all down in verse)

Sally started her day, on a pillow of hay,
and a nice cup of tea in the cover,
Served each day of the week, with a peck on the cheek,
by yours truly, her boyfriend and lover,
Now she's holding a broom, frittin from room to room,
with a duster and purpose in tow,
Having vacuumed the chairs, carpets, kitchen and stairs,
every room is beginning to glow,
As for mine, as I do, half past six on the loo,
could be six thirty-two at the most,
With my crossword and pen, which I do now and then,
plus, a hot cup of tea with some toast,
It's efficient no less, than my habit I guess,
in one door, out the other-a caper,
Then while still on the seat, and with crossword complete,
I then use it instead of loo-paper!

Was last Monday my friend, drove me up to attend,
an endoscope doctor and more,
There a camera as such, was shoved up my crutch,
which was painful, like never before,
To my loud screams and howls, they entered my bowels,
which I'm sure you would hear down in Devon,
It was driving me mad, Cos the camera they had,
was an old Kodak Brownie one seven,
On a serious note, from the surgeon to Quote,
it is clear, not all's well, down below,
And from what I have heard, I will soon be referred,
to a specialist, one who's in the know,
After taking a look, some biopsies were took,
but at least there was no cancer showing,
So regards what will be, it's still unknown to me,

so, let's say that the tests are on-going!

Ness has ants in her pants, she's gone over to France,
with the kids and has taken her car,
Staying there as a guest, with her in-laws in Brest,
which from Roscoff is not all that far,
She rang me last night, as a storm was in sight,
but remembering what advice she gave me,
I said not to fret, and that her best bet,
was to find and stand under a tree,
Tom and Sal, one and all, are down in Cornwall,
one assumes that they had a good trip,
No doubt a good cause, to help out with the chores,
for Sal's mother who's had a new hip,
Now Tom's not one to waste, or to act out in haste,
and the last to create any folly,
But if she starts to shout, if she can't get about,
I am sure Tom would make her a Trolley!

Now regards foreign lands, and our holiday plans,
it's confirmed, we are going its bingo,
Sally's Par-lay and voo-ing, Cava and is doing,
her best at translating the lingo,
Of course, I'm learning too, how to say "How d'you do"
in their accent with minimum fuss,
But there's no need to fret, because all those that I've met,
can speak far better English than us,
As for places to go, like the beach and Château,
of the former there's one for us each,
Golden sands mile on mile, sea as blue as the Nile,
little islands offshore within reach,
And of castles pray note, most of them have a moat,
and will look nothing less than quite grand,
Those I saw were all made, with a bucket and spade,
and constructed of nothing but sand!

Now where food is concerned, there's something I learned,
about Merv and his dietary needs,
I know that he's happy, to be rid of his nappy,
but he's still on the two-hourly feeds,
But in France the cuisine, is the best that I've seen,

69

and the choices are good I would say,
Plus, any time of the day, we can stop on our way,
for drinks at a roadside Café!
You will find that in France, there are fine restaurants,
where the service is first class as any,
And Creperies where, they serve pancakes in there,
and the types you can have they are many,
We could eat fairly well, at our local hotel,
but should it come down to the crunch,
I've just had a thought, as a final resort,
we could call in MacDonald's for lunch!

Verily 1st Earl of Runnymede

(The author and her husband like to visit their local bingo hall and felt the need to express the experience in a poem)

Bingo

We like a game of Bingo at our local Bingo Hall,
Eyes down look in and hope they call our balls.,
We're waiting for one number exciting it is too
We're hoping that the next ball out is number twenty-two.
OMG they've called it we shout with all our might,
Bingo, house, line, whatever comes out right!
We stop the bingo caller, who says that we have won,
What a nice surprise it is, she Says you've won a ton.
One hundred smackaroonies winning was a snip,
It will help to go towards, our next year's Switzerland trip.

Dora Blandford

The Birthday Card

(The author's sister once remarked to him, that she prefers chocolate to sex adding that at least she could remember what chocolate tastes like)

Tis I, your Baby Bro, the bard, the sender of this birthday card,
And if by you, perceived as nice, for me it has been worth the price,
And what a price, it wasn't cheap, for two nights Sue, I couldn't sleep,
But there again, lest I remiss, was worth it for my older sis,
Who cares dismay in fiscal matters, or a wallet left in tatters,
To give your birthday lots of bounce, and endless fizz what really counts,
So, no regrets from this 'ere chap, besides….I didn't want a slap.

They say when aged round sixty-five, most ladies seem to come alive,
Re-kindling, while old in tooth, the things they yearn, from early youth,
For some it's golf, for others drink, for some it's just a time to think,
For some a tartan Mini skirt, occasioning the chance to flirt,
For some reflecting suddenly, the loss of their virginity,
On this I'd say, don't bother Sue, if you know what's good for you,
Virginity for most a maid, was never lost, T'was just mislaid.

For OAPs there's always deals, snacks on tracks and Meals on Wheels,
Red Cross parcels, special seating, winter bonus for your heating,
Help the Aged, free prescriptions, free bus pass without restrictions,
Another thing which is a plus, is that when going on a bus,
Say if it's crowded and you mind, a vacant seat be hard to find,
There's always someone on who cares, enough to stand, and give you theirs,
Believe it Sue, it's not a lie, the same as pigs are known to fly.

Now that's the good news to be had, but be prepared to get the bad,
Being old is quite a strain, so expect yea, some aches and pain,
Diabetes, chronic stress, high blood pressure, I.B.S,
Short of breath a lack of sense, and maybe some incontinence,
Arthritic joints which causes groans, HRT and brittle bones,
Haemorrhoids which make you tense, and not forgetting flatulence,
Though methinks strongly of the latter, you're no stranger on that matter.

But for all that and finally, some kindly words, to you from me,
You're fit and well and fulsome too, and pray should live till ninety-
two,
And all there is for me to say, is I hope you have, a lovely day,
A jelly, more than just an eye-full, candle cake and whoppin' trifle,
Sweeties and some chocolate, which reminds me of your words of late,
True words they were, not said in haste, that at least you can recall the
taste! ! !

Verily 1st Earl of Runnymede

Old County Down

(The author, en-route to where he met and courted his wife, and where he regularly gave her flowers)

I'll be travelling this Friday, back to old County Down,
Visiting friends for the week, and of course Nanny Brown,
To Jerretzpass where, Diana once said,
I Do, in the church, where she and I wed,
I'll be giving out thanks, where they're needed in mind,
To those who've been helpful, so good and so kind,
But I'll also be seeking occasional pardons,
From all those in Newry, who kept such nice gardens,
They helped in my courtship, endless minutes and hours,
Unaware it was they, who supplied all my flowers

Verily 1st Earl of Runnymede

The Institution of Marriage

(The author's take on the pros and cons of marital life)

When two people marry, their lives and careers,
Are a mixture of cultures and both their ideas,
One ladylike finger, one masculine arm,
Individual habit and personal charm,
Plus, any ambition that either have got,
Is all melted down in the marital pot,
Now most would avoid, if they possibly could,
A chance that they might, be mis-understood,
But we all know it happens, it's one of those things,
It's one of the minefields, that married life brings,
For instance, TV, causes mostly dismay,
She wants East Enders, him match of the day,
In marriage for some it is so hard to please,
No matter which end of the toothpaste you squeeze,
To get over the hump, some need several shipments,
Of Sherpa's and oxygen and climbing equipment's,
But the best laugh of all, the bedroom's the place,
It's so very easy, for one to lose grace,
She's lying there keen, in the marital nest,
Smelling of perfume, and sexily dressed,
He's there in the bedroom, in old working clothes,
Scratching his bottom and picking his toes,
Now the girls too have moments, and you may give a cough,
But they have been known, to put a man off,
She doesn't mind sex, standing lying or sitting,
But hopes you won't mind, if she carries on knitting,
And how many times does she say, "Take me honey"
Followed by "Darling, I've run out of money"
But for all of these pitfalls, believe me it's true,
You cannot go wrong, if you just say "I do"

Verily 1st Earl of Runnymede

A Poorly Sis

(The author tries to cheer up his poorly sister)

Alas it was, my heart it fell, on hearing that, you were not well,
Not strong enough to use the phone, and call your brother up in Stone,
No energy to use a mop, or catch the bus and have a shop,
At pains to cook, no appetite, at best a sip, or just a bite,
And when I learnt you'd had a shower, which took you more than half
an hour,
I prayed aloud, oh dear God please, what's brought my big sis to her
knees,
And a voice boomed out, she's bound to wilt, because of all her
Childhood guilt.

I know the doctor's been on hand, and MRI scans have been planned,
You've had the Ultra-sound but then, they were not sure the why's and
when,
I know that Jools and Katie too, are helpful and been good to you,
Of late I know, RP I learned, has visited and been concerned,
And Tamzie too be in despair, to know her Gran is worse for wear,
Of course, I have my worries and, please know that I am close at hand,
To chauffeur you down to the quack, oh and to get my dust sheets
back.

I've pondered daily what could be, the cause of your infirmity,
A tummy bug or painful gout, some flatulence that can't get out,
Maybe shingles, scurvy, scabies, rheumatism, rickets rabies,
Things that cause a lack of smiles, like polyps, pimples, painful piles,
Or maybe something that you ate, an overdose of chocolate,
The cold, the wind, the air, the heat, a poison caused by rancid meat,
Mosquito bite, but if that's true, it's sure to be as ill as you.

Well anyway, regarding plans, I'm sure you're in Professional hands,
And in no time are sure to be, back on your feet and fancy free,
Up the garden, reading books, comfy chair and sun-tan looks,
Holidays, back in top gear, for fifty-one weeks of the year,
Lozzicking on Spanish Visas, eating Mars Bars and Maltesers,
Sunday roasts with apple tart, or even better A la' Carte,
But until then, I'm sure you know, get well from me, your Baby Bro.

Verily 1st Earl of Runnymede

The Astral Clock

(The author here gives a short instruction on how to calculate the time by using the stars)

If you're travelling at night, on foot or in cars,
~~You might care to gaze, in the sky at the stars,~~
You'll not only see a fine view in it's prime,
But a way to find out, where you are and the time,
You'll be needing a bob weight, just something to dangle,
And something to measure, a mean obtuse angle,
Not much training is needed, that is understood,
But your Astral Chronology's got to be good,

March the 7th at midnight is what you'd expect,
The clock in the heavens, is true and correct,
You've some time to deduct, though don't ask me why,
For it gains by 2 hours, for each month that goes by,
The clock has one hand, two stars you will see,
You call them the Pointers, appropriately,
You'll not hear a tick and you'll not hear a tock,
But the Pole star's the centre, of your Astral clock.

Way above of the pole star, is midnight (The moon)
And directly below it, the skyline is noon,
Due left of the pole star, in case you don't know,
Is 0600hrs, when the cock starts to crow,
Due right of the pole star, at similar height,
Is where the hands are, at six every night,
Good plotting, good clocking, wherever you roam,
And you should be on time when you finally get home

Verily 1st Earl of Runnymede

Love

Love can be cruel, and love can be kind,
But when you find it, don't leave it behind.
Feelings are strong, emotions are high.
It's hard to let it just go by.

You're hit by the arrow of cupid's bow.
Once you have found it, don't let it go.
The nerves in your tummy, the spark in your mind.
Love is a special thing; you don't often find.

Your heart skips a beat, whenever you meet
The two of you can't be apart.
From the very first day, I just wanted to say.
I will love you with all of my heart.

Dora Blandford

The Blackpool Lights

(The author has a night out in Blackpool with friends)

On one September Saturday, a friend and I we went away,
To Blackpool where, with worries gone, the sky was blue, the sun it
shone,
To walk from Starr-Gate parking lot, on sea front, which was just so
hot,
For luncheon fayre if not so finer, than a sea front open diner,
Bacon cheese in toasted bread, two cups of slush, one blue, one red,
We ordered few chips on our plate, were served up nigh, a
hundredweight,
And thus, with waistlines out of reach, we headed for the Pleasure
Beach.

We rumbled on the Gold mine train, our search for nuggets was in
vain,
A fruitless task, it seemed a lark, we found none as, it was too dark,
The next ride which from us got praise, was round the world in eighty
days,
But splashing water, knew no end, it was just like, a wet weekend,
We entered then, just for a change, a house said to be very strange,
Plasma balls and mirrors plied, amazing things were found inside,
No more than when, with feet on ground, the room we went in, spun
right round.

But then for laughs, with tickets bought, and feeling brave, this time we
caught,
The Ghost Train shunting from the halt, we took it with a pinch of salt,
That was until, they dimmed the light, I got a glimpse, a gruesome
sight,
Was there in full view, made me swoon, the creature from the black
lagoon,
An awesome, ugly, grotesque figure, I bit my nails and screamed with
vigour,
But then when close I got a clue, then a mirror came in view,
The ultra-frightening, awesome ghoulie, I realised, was just yours truly.

Was then day's end, indeed was dark, back to the car there at the park,
Then drove along to see the sights, provided by the Blackpool lights,
Cinderella, Robin Hood, Pinocchio, Babes in the Wood,
Toadstools, Daleks, streamers, tassels, bright enchanted magic castles,
Pirate ships and holy grails, and other things from fairy Tales,
It was a great, fantastic show, but was for us, the time to go,
Indeed, it was in every way, a pleasant and rewarding day.

Verily 1st Earl of Runnymede

My Hero Woody

(The author, ex Guards makes sarcastic jibes at a fellow colleague who is an ex-Royal Marine)

I've shaved my head completely, and now I wear a tie,
Press my trousers daily, and here's the reason why,
They call it hero worship, you know what I mean,
I wanna be like Woody, cause he's an ex-Marine !

I don't now wear a jumper, although we're in mid-winter,
And I never use a plaster when I get a cut or splinter,
I now sleep with the lights off, and sing "God save the Queen"
Just to be like Woody, cause he's an ex-Marine !

I used to buy the Telegraph, but then I heard it said,
Marines were not that literate, so I get the Star instead,
And I struggle with the crossword, like a man who lacks the means,
And all to be like Woody, cause he's an ex-Marine !

Verily 1st Earl of Runnymede

Tablets

(This was sent to a woman, along with some painkillers after her discharge from hospital)

With aims to your comfort, and noble intent,
Please find enclosed, all the tablets I've sent,
I'm sure you'll agree, there is more than you'll need,
But please do be careful, and dosage rate heed,
When a headache comes on, and your head's like a vice,
Just half a tablet, should more than suffice,
For migraines that linger, and if giving grief,
A whole tablet taken, will give some relief,
For backache and toothache, old war wounds and flu',
It is best if you take, maybe no more than two,
If you've aching sore sides, after starting to laugh,
The dosage rate here, is just two and a half,
For hangovers, gout, or if stung by a bee,
You can increase the dosage, and take up to three,
For wounds to the body, which are tender and sore,
The tablets you take, should be no more than four,
But. . .
If your husband can't sleep, and he drops being formal,
You notice he's smiling and warmer than normal,
He's friendly and playful and scratching his chin,
Wants to go to bed early and wearing a grin,
Just say you feel rough and a headache is lurking,
And for some unknown reason, the tablets aren't working.

Verily 1st Earl of Runnymede

Never forget how to Laugh

(Some advice from a well-travelled author)

Clairvoyantly, it's plain to see, as time unlocks the door,
That inclement climes, and troubled times, is what we have in store,
And the answer to the question, as to what we are to do,
I' have to voice, we have no choice, our options are so few,
But perceiving all around me, with a clear and vivid sight,
I came to a conclusion, which I'm confident is right.
You can say we're at the mercy, of the lord regards our health,
At the mercy of designer goods, regards our means and wealth,
And woe betide the poor in each, with little dues to spend,
For those who have invested well, but reaped no dividend,
The cards of life are random, dealt a hand you're rich or poor,
Luck cannot be reserved as such, it's only by the draw,
But not matter what life deals you, don't play your cards by half,
Be slave or king, forget anything, but never, how to laugh.

Verily 1st Earl of Runnymede

84

Competition

(The author organised a puzzle-in-a-bottle for charity by offering £5
for anyone who can work out who Verily was)

Your imagination was I hope, in gear and at full throttle,
When you found this note, a verse or two, contained here in this bottle,
You see this poem has some clues, and if you are fair wise,
There is the chance that you could win, another humble prize.

The rules are very simple, and herein lies the key,
All you have to do is find the person known as Verily,
That's all you've got to work out, just call him night or day,
And he will give you £5 from his wallet straight away.

Verily, he plays guitars, he's been around on stage,
For thirteen years a soldier, that's how he earned his wage,
For years an electrician, and here I have to grin,
He wired St John's some time ago, the church you're standing in.

Verily loves Christmas, he's happiest at that,
He likes to see the Christmas tree and wear his Santa hat,
He watches out for Santa and listens for the door,
And you'll find him in the window, of the house you're looking for.

And finally, I hope you see, and here I do admit,
The prize is no great fortune, indeed or part of it,
But in good faith I am hoping, in the spirit that was done,
That if nothing else in finding me, you have a bit of fun !

Verily 1st Earl of Runnymede

85

The Special Wedding

(The author is invited to a very special occasion, the wedding of his cousin and co-author)

It is with joy, I'd like to say, I hope you'll like your special day,
The marriage rites embraced by you, resulting in a loud "I do"
Conforming with formality, surrounded by your family,
Plus, all your friends who cannot wait, to wish you well and celebrate,
Brothers, sisters, Auntie Betty, throwing heaps of white confetti,
Blushing bride and groom so dashing, posing for the cameras flashing,
Then driving off in limousine, for welcome drink and fine cuisine !

Invited guests, as you draw near, as protocol demands will hear…
"Pray be upstanding, all in room, to warmly welcome bride and groom"
You'll take your seats, they'll be the best, then followed sharply by each guest,
To each a fayre, fit for a king, from kitchen will the waiters bring,
Then wedding speeches of the day, when he, the groom can have his say,
And others too who wish to spice, proceedings with some sound advice,
Which you may take, or put away, until required some other day !

And then the hour, to don the gown, take jacket off and let hair down,
On the dance floor, people hopping, to the sound of wine corks popping,
Drinks a flowing, champagne hissing, music playing, bridesmaids kissing,
People who have chose to bless, with values we call happiness,
The marriage of two souls for life, a good man and his loyal wife,
And so, for me, on this your day, there is but one thing left to say,
Congratulations, as one does, with lots of love from me, your Cuz !

Verily 1ˢᵗ Earl of Runnymede

(The Author has an African Grey Parrot)

My African Grey Parrot

I have a little parrot; his name is Rudolf see,
I share my breakfast toast with him, and he says Hello to me.
He dances to some funky tunes, gets right into the groove.
You should see him go you know, he's s really got the moves.
He whistles Adams family, and he phones auntie Eve.
He even calls the dogs, when he sees them on TV!
He is the cat detective, when he sees a puss outside.
He screams and makes a song and dance, that we just can't abide.
He's a noisy little parrot, when we are on the phone,
I couldn't live without him; I would feel so all alone.
I've had him over thirty years, a long long time you see.
I love him so very much; he means the world to me.

Dora Blandford

Thoughts of Autumn

I awoke with the dawn, rubbed my eyes, had a yawn,
Dressed and hurried downstairs with some fizz,
Went outdoors for a joke, rolled a fag, had a smoke,
And sat thinking how nice autumn is,
Autumn colours behold, yellows, brown, red and gold,
All displaying a wonderful view,
Just seeing the trees, brought my thoughts to their knees,
So, I thought I would share them with you.

For a walk and a lark, I would go to the park,
Up by keepers and through the woods there,
Seeing beeches well thinned, by the autumnal wind,
Leaving all of the branches quite bare,
Falling leaves from on high, as I trundled on by,
Like confetti at any proud weddin'
Kicking leaves as you do, but with dog toilets few,
I was mindful of what I might tread in!

Thoughts of past reddened knuckles, caused by conkers brought
chuckles,
Of schooldays remembered with passions,
Finding chestnuts around, after searching the ground,
As a way of improving my rations,
Eating brambles galore, killed off hunger and more,
But the downside was "iffy" it's true,
With each handful you take, you could get tummy ache,
And could spend half the night on the Loo!

Now September's impressed, with a colourful guest,
Which is hardy to all types of weather,
Giving radiant hue, in mauve, purple and blue,
And of course, I'm referring to Heather,
If it's white so they say, good luck comes your way,
Maybe so but to me that is strange,
For I once bought a pose, from a Gypsy called Rose,
And she left without giving me change!

After autumn expires, you start to light fires,
To keep the cold winter at bay,
Snow and ice, wind and rain, 'till the spring comes again,
Which arrives in the last week of May,
But I beg don't despair, or start pulling your hair,
And pray, keeps your hopes in good focus
For you just never know, when we're rid of the snow,
I may well write of Snowdrops and Crocus!

Verily 1ˢᵗ Earl of Runnymede

Scafell Pike

(The author climbed England's highest mountain and left this poem at the summit)

'Tis grand, to stand, atop as planned, the highest mountain in the land,
Challenging, a Christian host, providing views of distant coast,
Below behold, green, open wide, a view inducing personal pride,
Rich dividends, await those boots, who've come to muse, their English
roots,
From here all climbers realise, the kingdom it personifies,
A nation proud, a nation free, with honour, and with dignity,
It stirs the heart like none before, fills every mountaineer with awe,
Yes, Scafell Pike does much impress, all those who value Englishness.

If anyone, were wanting proof, to stand atop of England's roof,
In making claim and proving worth, just point to anywhere on earth,
There is no sea, no ocean blue, the ensign has not sailed on through,
Sons of England, jolly tars, navigating by the stars,
Seamen worth another look, epitomised by Captain Cook,
They gambled all in Captains cap, to add more place names to the map,
Dropping anchor, reaching sands, in far and distant foreign lands,
Exporting freely at a guess, the value we call Englishness.

And what of those in war who diced, who bravely fought and
sacrificed,
Not only those who manned the fleet, to save the country from defeat,
But soldiers unafraid to bleed, enlisting in the hour of need,
Contemptibles with gun and bomb, who fought the Hun upon the
Somme,
And countless other battles he, engaged to save democracy,
Old soldiers now, who are denied, the ones who bravely fought and
died,
Would gladly suffer all that pain, to stand where you are, once again,
Their finest hour was more or less, the value we call Englishness.

'Tis grand, to stand, atop as planned, the highest mountain in the land,
I take a breath, the air is sweet, with all of England at my feet,
I owe my country much I say, indeed far more than I could pay,
I see this kingdom, much my own, and Scafell Pike it's mighty throne,
'Tis more than just a climb to bridge, for Englishmen, it's pilgrimage,
A place to think, what you'd expect, a place for prayer and to reflect,
And really all of that's not odd, up here you're closer to your God,
T'was he who chose this place to Bless, with values we call Englishness.

Verily 1st Earl of Runnymede

The Toby Jugs in town.

(The author sent his mother in law a Toby Jug and she started collecting them)

They say that Toby Jugs are rare, and rightly so I fear,
It seems they leave the mainland, and simply disappear,
The authorities were worried, were the Russians playing tricks,
So, they brought in Scotland yard with the help of MI6,
But they only had one suspect, her name was Nanny Brown,
She had the best collection, of Toby Jugs in town.

They asked around the county, but nobody would sing,
Each question it was answered with "I haven't seen a thing"
But a postman out delivering, in Bessbrook for a while,
Said he'd seen a good few parcels, and each was marked Fragile,
He wouldn't give a postcode, but he said "Find nanny Brown"
She's got the best collection, of Toby Jugs in town.

The search team looked through windows, and all at once they saw,
A one-eyed Pirate Toby Jug, and several hundreds more,
There was one of Ali Babba, there was one of old John Bull,
In the living room they noticed that the dresser, it was full,
One said "I know who lives here, her name is Nanny Brown"
She's got the best collection of Toby Jugs in town.

Now the moral of this story, is not what you expect,
It's not a case of what you know, but more what you collect,
Some people gather foreign coins, antiques, a book, a stamp,
But when it comes to Toby Jugs, there only is one Champ,
Miss Toby Jug her title, her name is Nanny Brown,
She's got the best collection, of Toby Jugs in town.

Verily 1st Earl of Runnymede

A Brotherly Prescription

(Knowing his sister to be poorly, the author took her some chocolate)

Knowing wisely on visits, you have placed an embargo,
This page was delivered, by hand with its cargo,
And a pretty nice cargo indeed I must add,
Which compared to a laxative, isn't all bad,
Of medicinal value, as far as it goes,
Methinks you will find, that the contents enclosed,
Although hardly effectual in fighting disease,
Tastes better than Aspirin, and has been known to please,
Of proverbial worth, you will know of the phrase,
When taking prescriptions, with sugar it pays,
To weaken a spoonful, alleviates frown,
Makes it taste better, when getting it down,
And whilst mindful the contents, is not sugar cane,
I just can't imagine, that you will complain.

Verily 1st Earl of Runnymede

93

The Midland Mountaineers

(Some of the author's family – Gemma, Sian, Sue, Kate,
Tamzin and RP, Climb Mount Snowdon with him)

Was a Friday in Wales, during rain, hail and gales,
with a forecast as grim as was true.
Notwithstanding the wet, all us mountaineers met,
in a car park which featured a loo.
That indeed was a treat, for the girls on their feet,
one I'd say was as good as was any.
Gemma, Sian, Sue and Kate, well they just couldn't wait,
when they got there to each spend a Penny!

Now we set off that day, Tamzin leading the way,
with the pace I would say fairly quick.
But we didn't get far, I went back to the car,
as poor Gran had forgotten her stick.
Now I'm not one to gloat, but it's worth taking note,
pray I'm hoping you'll all grin and bear it.
For I hasten to add, not a broomstick I'm glad,
but if the hat fits … you can wear it!

Round about ten o'clock, by the large Gladstone rock,
the disaster, what we'd all been loathing.
Though was dry in the main, well it started to rain,
So, we all donned our waterproof clothing.
I saw from, where I stood, Gemma wearing a hood,
and believe me I started to fret.
I'm not saying at all, that she's tiny or small,
but she had to run round to get wet!

At say 2,000 feet, we all sat down to eat,
it was then Stevie Wonder appeared.
With a dog on a lead, it was then we agreed,
that the man and his dog both looked weird.
Plus, he warned we'd not cope, on the last final slope,
but his words I found empty and sparse.
Was unhelpful and so, I told him he could go,
and could stick his advice up his armpit!

Now I knew in my heart, that the difficult part,
was the last five or six hundred feet.
Even stooping to crawl, one can easily fall,
that's where so many climbers get beat.
And I'm sure you'll have guessed, I was deeply impressed,
seeing Grandma climb up, it was funny.
Being helped I could see, by no less than RP,
it's surprising what he'll do for money!

Though we'd paid a high price, on the top it was nice,
and our thanks go to Katie for tea.
Thanks to Gem for the treat, when she fell from her seat,
and the Farley's Rusks courtesy of me.
Was a much welcome break, but we'd footprints to make,
and admittedly wearing a frown.
We left the Café, and we then made our way,
to the path which would take us back down.

When we got to the park, it was really quite dark,
and we all were so tired and wet.
But although we were spent, we had made an ascent,
by the longest and hardest route yet.
As for me I can say, was a wonderful day,
though right now I'm so stiff and in pain.
Giving credit where due, it was all thanks to you,
So, my thanks to you all once again!

Verily 1st Earl of Runnymede

The Birds and Bees

(A slightly buttered but nonetheless true story, of one of the author's schoolboy ventures)

When I was just a young lad, I'd say about fourteen,
I got around to thinking, of things I hadn't seen,
I wasn't sure what they were but, my life had something missing,
Us boys were playing football, but the girls were out there kissing,
So, petitioning my father, I got down on my knees,
And asked him if he'd tell me, all about the birds and bees.

He said … the girls you will have noticed son, are shaped quite
differently,
They're curvy and more rounded, compared to you and me,
In girls you'll find emotions, gravity and stresses,
And ferrets fighting one another, underneath their dresses,
Now if you're a mind to sample son, a taste of milk and honey,
The ladies are expensive, so make sure you've got some money.

So, I called for my old schoolboy chum, a lad of similar feather,
Him and I were great friends, and went everywhere together,
With our wages from our paper rounds, we'd enough to oil our loins,
This amounted to a ten bob note and several foreign coins,
So, armed with what Dad taught me, of the Ladies Highway Code,
We caught the bus to Birmingham and went to Varna Road.

There was juicy Lucy, handy Anne, slack Alice and Godiva,
Along with willing Jill, who were going for a fiver,
Miss Bondage and Miss Whiplash, and the famed Miss Fancy free,
Who were slightly more expensive, as they all charged v.a.t,
Unruly Julie, Pat the cat and bargains to be found,
With some you'd get some change, if you paid them with a pound.

I plucked up courage, took the plunge, and said "Excuse me miss"
It's just my mate was wondering, what you'd charge him for a kiss,
    She answered quite seductively and said "That all depends,
    On the size of your mate's engine, his piston and big ends"
I said "It's not my business, you can charge him what you like"
    But he hasn't got a license, let alone a motorbike.

    The hour was late, we'd had our fun, was time for us to fly,
    But my schoolboy chum insisted, on a last and final try,
    This time he did the talking, to a girl I heard him say,
    "I'll let you read my Beano, if you let us have our way"
    While thankful for the offer, of the comic that he'd bought,
    She said "I could be tempted" but I read the Sunday Sport"

Verily 1st Earl of Runnymede

97

(The Author thoughts on getting through the working day)

A working life

Get up in the morning, jump up out of bed.
Facing the workload, of the day ahead.
You find it too hard, with pressure and stress.
Think! Slow down, breath, and progress.
Friends make it easier, to get through your day.
With fun and some laughter, to help earn your pay.
Go home get the dinner on, it's now time to eat.
Relax and chill out, it's time for some sleep.

Dora Blandford

Impressions of a Mid-week Break

(The author goes on a weekend break to Wales, but rain stopped play)

The homes of landed gentry squires, cathedrals with the tallest spires,
Gardens where one sits for hours, immersed in pastel coloured flowers,
Pubs for tasty evening meals, patchwork quilts of farmers' fields,
Saxon Churches, added knaves, in the churchyard ancient graves,
And therein suffered natures pain, with two days of torrential rain!

Well-trodden paths and loose stone walls, forests green and waterfalls,
Castles massive, castles lesser, built by Edward the Confessor,
Forty different coloured grasses, mountain peaks and mountain passes,
Torrents walk where one needs talents, if one is, to keep one's balance,
We saw a few but in the main, we couldn't see for all the rain!

Atlantic rollers, gentle surf, sand dunes topped with rye grass turf,
The harbour lights, the buoys the floats, the bridge, the nets, the fishing
boats,
The ice cream stalls, the shops, the fair, to breathe the healthy seaside air,
Miles of beach, a sight so grand, to run barefooted in the sand,
We could have both been kids again, but couldn't due to all that rain!

Forest roads long swept away, over bridges where you pay,
In cash or currency that's hard, and not in kind or Barclaycard,
Workings mined by Romans old, who left a trail of lead and gold,
Prospecting along the road, and Thomas Grey's Alcaic Ode,
By then we'd water on the brain, all thanks to nothing else but rain!

We'll go again when summer's burst, but next time check the weather first,
To walk that cliff, and laze the beach, and do things that were out of reach,
We'll slowly walk through forests old, we'll take potluck and pan for gold,
We'll ride that pony though the fells, and on that island gather shells,
Next time we go we'll not refrain, and hopefully, we'll miss the rain!

Verily 1st Earl of Runnymede

Interesting Subjects

(One of those days when the author had nothing else to write about)

Academics, arthritis, the Incas, Peru,
geography, history to name but a few,
Of subjects on offer, of daughters and dance,
of boyfriends and girlfriends, of love and romance,
Of narrow escapes, of futures and plans,
sons who've gone skiing, and Rock 'n Roll bands,
Of bullets and bullies, the snow, endless showers,
of loneliness, heartache, of upset for hours,
Of ponies and horses, of buses and cars,
pianos and trumpets and 6 string guitars,
Of mothers and fathers, of sisters no less,
And those in your life, who have served to impress,
Of soft Irish accents, good friendships that last,
parachutes, pupils, mistakes in the past,
Of hardships and heartache, endured when young,
of speaking hard German, and gentle French tongue,
Of Tigers, Orangutans, far distant lands,
using eyes to express, what you can't with your hands,
Faeroe's, Viking, Cromarty, forty, Children being very naughty,
Of merchants, mechanics, of millers and miners,
restaurants and Bistros, small café's and diners,
Of Scotland and whiskey and Harris Isle tweeds,
Lincoln and London, Liverpool, Leeds,
Your garden at home and what's in it that's growing,
mortgages and, any money that's owing,
The general election, an old piece of rope,
your neighbours, a budgie, a pencil, the Pope,
The Grenadier Guards, best stand up and salute,
an account overdrawn or a wellington boot,
Some plaster of Paris, a castle you made,
on the beach at the seaside with bucket and spade,
A teapot, your auntie, the shoes you've had mended,
not speaking to someone because you're offended,
Reading the paper or just playing conkers,
talking to someone who you think is bonkers,
Or reading this verse if you have time to spend,
from a poet in Stone. . . who was at a loose end.

Verily 1st Earl of Runnymede

The Unwanted Toby Jug

(The author buys an unwanted Toby Jug from a car boot sale for his mother in law)

This sorry, sad, crestfallen tale, began at Sunday's car boot sale,
For bargain hunters fresh from slumbers, turned out in sufficient numbers,
With ready cash and wallets willing, they all were out, to make a killing,
Figurines with rosy cheeks, medals, coins and rare antiques,
Writing desks in marquetry, rare books and old jewellery,
Dealers caught on fast enough, scooped up the rare and first-class stuff,
They bought the Rembrandts feeling smug, but chose to leave the Toby Jug.

This Toby Jug was not the best, the dealers they, were not impressed,
They knew and sadly would agree, it bore no makers pedigree,
No wonder it had not been sold, it wasn't from a Wedgewood mould,
Nor Dresden china, Wade or Ming, in name it wasn't worth a thing,
Its colours too, although in glaze, it's true they had seen better days,
He's been on sale at special price, some looked at it, but never twice,
It seemed this Toby Jug so old, was destined never, to be sold.

A Gent he stopped, and then he took, a long and interested look,
He saw the blue, the black and grey, and other colours on display,
He picked him up and saw that on, the base the name engraved was John,
He pondered, thinking for a while, and soon the gent began to smile,
The Toby Jug that he just saw, is just what he'd been looking for,
The gent he said I think he's nice, I want him so, just name your price,
I'm sending him to County Down, like all the rest, to Nanny Brown.

Verily 1st Earl of Runnymede

A Day Climbing

(The author took a somewhat portly friend to North Wales for the day, a walk was planned but the friend insisted on climbing a mountain as he'd never climbed one before, the author agreed and took him up mount Snowdon)

With aims to rest a troubled mind, to make it clear and strong,
I headed for a gold mine, and I took a friend along,
I'd planned a walk, through forests old, a stroll I'd contemplated,
But was unaware my friend, and Sherpa Tensing were related,
He said the walk, it sounded nice, and peaceful as it were,
But to climb a granite mountain was, what he would much prefer,
I warned inclement weather, and the dangers of pneumonia,
But my friend he wasn't daunted, so we headed for Snowdonia.

The ground was awful boggy, we couldn't park on grass,
So, we paid to use the car park, built atop Llanberis Pass,
We set off with a vengeance, for I knew which way to go,
I was leading from the front, my friend I had in tow,
When I heard a voice behind me, out of breath and in despair,
Was my friend who had been asking me if we were nearly there,
I clearly had a problem, but thought wise not to fret,
I said now don't be silly, we've not left the car park yet !

When we reached above three thousand feet, I'd say in not bad time,
I knew we only had about, 500 feet to climb,
So, I turned around to tell him, which would fill him with delight,
But instead I saw him struggling, in a very sorry sight,
He was steaming like a sauna, his clothes were dripping wet,
His lungs were working overtime, his pockets full of sweat,
With aims kind to encourage, I could not resist to say,
And told him he had made it to, a point about halfway!

Well we reached the summit safely, and that's where my friend found,
That it's best when throwing snowballs, if you take the higher ground,
But that was only schoolboy stuff and here I have to say,
How nice it was his company, out climbing for the day,
And we plan to hit North Wales again, although he's made some changes,
I cannot see us heading for the hills and mountain ranges,
He's had it with high altitude, and thinks his new career,
In search of gold, through forests old, ain't such a bad idea!

Verily 1st Earl of Runnymede

The Innocence of Youth

(On taking my infantile nephew and son to the public conveniences, I boldly told them both of the pecking order to be followed, namely that the big boys go on the right, and the little boys go to the left, but my words were misinterpreted with comical results and they took it that I meant their height. Years later on the day my nephew married, the following was read out to the guests attending his wedding reception)

Now here's a little story, I'll tell you if I may,
About the groom, that's in this room, whilst on a holiday,
That's Steve of course but also, he was with my son and I,
On forest trails, up in North Wales, beneath a clear blue sky,
We'd had methinks, too many drinks, and thus it made good sense,
To look around, until we found, a signpost for the Gents,
And it didn't take us too long, 'fore we found one good as any,
Then Tom and Steve and I with aims, went off to spend a penny,
Inside the place we lined up, as us boys are known to do,
Me on the right, but then caught sight, of both the other two,
I said now hang on fellas, you're in danger of disgrace,
You can't just stand, and go as planned, you have to take your place,
The big boys take the right-hand spot, it's prudent and it's wise,
It's more a case, you take your place, according to your size,
It was nothing but pure banter, and I'm sure you will agree,
But Steve then pushed Tom to one side and stood there next to me,
I looked at Steve quite puzzled, for I'd not yet seen him peek,
And after all the words I'd said, were spoken tongue in cheek,
So, I asked Steve to explain himself, as uncles often do,
He said Tom's only three foot six..... and I'm nearly four foot two.

Verily 1st Earl of Runnymede

Saying it

(Advice for budding suitors on Valentine's day)

You could say it with flowers, a gorgeous bouquet,
You could say it with chocolates, a box of milk tray,
You could say it with perfume, a bottle of scent,
Or say it in verse, and she'll know what was meant,
You could shout from a mountain, with aims to endear,
A noble intention, but doubtful she'll hear,
Leave a message of love, what girl would want more,
With ribbons and rosettes, tied to her front door,
But the best way to make a girl feel like a girl,
Make her heart skip a beat and make all her toes curl,
Pray forget cultured pearls, or the romantic Latin,
The best way of all…. is to say it with Satin.

Verily 1st Earl of Runnymede

(The Author and her husband, who are keen followers of anything astronomical, followed Tim Peake's adventure to the International Space Station)

Astronaut

Tim Peake in a rocket he's travelling into space,
A very excited spaceman, first Britain to win the race.
space station destination passing layers as he goes,
Into Orbit is the next bit, it keeps him on his toes.
The capsule is arriving, and ready now to dock.
Twists and turns precisely, a button pressed to lock.
He's floating in the station meeting up with all the crew.
I'm a British spaceman, and ready to work with. you.
Around the world in ninety-two minutes, it's going around so fast.
Looking out the window, taking photos as it passed.
It's seen from Earth at certain times, we watch it go right by.
A tiny light just like a star, zooming through the sky.
In Orbit for a long time, ran a marathon he's very clever.
Back on Earth and landed, that was the best ride ever.

Dora Blandford

The Party

(The author and his girlfriend are invited to a fancy-dress party and sent the following acceptance)

We were having our breakfast, that is Sally and me,
Nothing special, just cornflakes and a hot cup of tea,
Indulging the marmalade, on hot buttered toast,
When your letter arrived, through my door in the post,
'Twas your kind invitation, what a lovely surprise,
And yes, we'll be there, and this time in disguise.

Now we've given much thought, to what we should wear,
But we've hit a brick wall, and we're now in despair,
Sally was saying, how nice 'twould have been,
If I dressed as Napoleon, and she, Josephine,
But I had to decline, robbing Sally of smiles,
For Sal can't speak French, and me . . . I've no piles.

Busy thinking of couples, who we could have been,
From Starsky and Hutch, to Torville and Dean
There was Batman and Robin, always getting in fights,
But Sally's no boxer, and I look daft in tights,
Godiva was mentioned, (with underwear of course)
A great part for Sal, but I can't be a horse.

There was Big Ears and Noddy, now that sounded good,
Sally dressed all in green, with a pointed red hood,
But me wearing two massive ears made no sense,
With the danger that someone, could well take offence,
Tongues might get poked out, harsh words come to pass,
Even worse he might stuff both the ears up my . .Armpit.

Though both undecided, we aim to impress,
Turning up bearing gifts and be in fancy dress,
I might be Bin-Laden, and Sal Britney Spears,
The only thing I'm sure of is, I won't be wearing ears,
So, if two strangers turn up, dressed up and fancy free,
Please don't send them packing cos. . . . . it might be Sal and Me.

Verily 1st Earl of Runnymede

To an old friend

(The author sends this to one of his old army friends)

Now a call to an old friend, indeed it makes sense,
but in view of the distance and awesome expense,
My wallet it trembled and started to stall,
so, my thanks for returning, my original call.
It was so good to chuckle and yet I must add,
we spoke only a fraction, of the good times we had,
Out East in Malaysia, two years in Paroi,
To be fair at eighteen, I was only a boy,
Of aforementioned hardship, low income and pay,
the disciplined life, plus a hard-working day,
Then our time in the jungle, by Christ it was rough,
mosquitoes and snakes, rhino beetles and stuff,
The barracks was home for us lads in the Guards,
Marching around, shooting guns, playing cards,
With the trumpeter blowing at dawn every morning,
but was drowned out by sounds, of the garrison yawning,
Devious flankers and stunts we would pull,
to stave spit and polish and similar bull,
But instead of complaining to senior staff,
we made good the shortfall, by having a laugh.
So, let us make space and meet up at last,
Lest our laughter becomes, just a thing of the past.

Verily 1st Earl of Runnymede

107

A Happy Occasion

(The author is away on holiday but left this for his sister)

On this happy occasion, I thought that I might, with a view to
updating, in verse that I'd write,
Notwithstanding the fact being written in most, by a long absent
brother and sent in the post,
For upon this receipt, I am distant not nearer, and by now on a beach
towel, in sunny Madeira,
With my girlfriend no less, than a maiden so fine, who's hand can be
found, most the time inside mine,
And as I'm away on the day of your birth, coupled with the fact I, am a
brother of worth,
I have sat and composed, having thought now and then, for I know
you're a fan, of my capable pen.

Happy Birthday indeed, and my greetings to you, fairest of all my
sisters, and oldest one too,
But that wasn't your fault, was the war, was the norm, it was mum's
black suspenders, and Dad's uniform,
Were conceived I should think, pray I've harboured the thought, it
must've been in, an air-raid shelter of sort,
Which explains why you're constantly digging in earth, like the Salmon
returning to the place of its birth,
And another thing here, I remember some nights, you blinked several
times, when I turned on the lights,
A marked indication, what now is a thorn, for was during the "Black-
out" you must have been born .

Yes, you've been there and done it, oozed blood sweat and tears, and
now wearing a Tee shirt of 63 years,
The senior sibling, of Ma' George's three, you being the eldest, the
youngest is me,
Now it's hard to remember that quite Spartan era, while sunning
oneself on the coast of Madeira,
Though I'd never forget as a very small mister, living in constant fear,
of a much older sister,

108

But as it's your birthday, I want you at last, to know I forgive you for all
that is past,
Plus, I'd like to say sorry, and ask for your pardon, for burying your
tadpoles, deep in the back garden.

Thus, there only remains, my kind wishes to pay, on this special
occasion, and such happy day,
And as your baby bro' who, now lives off a pension, I thought would
be nice, I occasioned a mention,
To say you're good looking, you've charm and have wits, and clearly
well blessed with a great pair of knees,
You can still touch your toes, no mean feat say your peers, unlike me
who has not seen his own for some years,
A brilliant cook too, if a comment pass may, but not least a small
tribute I wanted to say,
And that's please find enclosed, a few pennies to spend, for not only a
sister, you're a wonderful friend.

Verily 1st Earl of Runnymede

The Family

(The author writes a description of his family)

It's Saturday evening, having dined we're at rest, that's the family and Sally , who's here as a guest,

And I thought early on, just how nice it would be, if I gave her some tips, regards our family,

Now there's only one lady in charge of the manor, my wife and a mother, her name is Diana,

Her dreams are unique during most of her slumbers, but as yet she has failed, with the lottery numbers,

She was one of four daughters, her dad felt despair, after Diana was born he lost most his hair,

Now the funny thing is, and it's strange you'll agree, I also lost mine, after she married me.

There's my daughter Vanessa who you've already met, she's not frightened of water until she gets wet,

On a walk in the dark she's courageous and wise, with one arm out in front, and one covering her eyes,

She's a talented artist and cook is our Ness, but it takes half the evening to clear up the mess,

When Ness was at home it was wonderful bliss, but you don't know how grateful, I am now to Chris.

Chris is the son in law but in fairness you see, we think of him very much, as close family,

A whiz-kid on hard drive, a French ex-marine, but not fond of water as we've already seen,

On the seawall at Mullion, which was then all the rave, he got soaked head to foot by a gigantic wave,

Chris's face said it all, but I didn't gloat, at the time he was wearing, my best leather coat

Now Tom has always been keen on the stars, as a boy he would always be playing with cars,

But he had other hobbies, and was also dead keen, on breaking his curtains and mum's figurine,

He liked loosing car keys, going out for the day, of fishing for tiddlers with his friend called PK,

Recognising wildflowers, playing out in the snow, and often the blue bell woods would go,

Not forgetting poor granddad, he's family too, you can't hold him back, for he's too much to do,

Breakfast at seven, his lunch 12:15, even having a wee pray is done to routine,

He likes a long talk but it's sad that for years, granddad never got round, to using his ears,

Take a lift in his car, you'll be shaking for hours, and think that you're back, inside Alton Towers,

With respect to yours truly, there's less to reveal, a talented man, heart of gold, made of steel,

With rugged good looks, wits and charm, is the chat, and I'll let you work out, whose opinion is that.

Verily 1st Earl of Runnymede

Me

(A few lines about the author)

Now today's my day off, and thus I am free,
So I thought I would write, a few words about me,
Not everything pray but a few things to know,
And to start with I thought, I would just say hello,
Now I'm fairly laid back, of hang-ups I've none,
I'm normally happy, easy going and fun,
You'll not hear me swear, or e'er raise my voice,
I detest all things loud, disrespectful and coarse,
I'm tolerant, witty, I hold my friends dear,
Intelligent, helpful, forgiving, sincere,
Hard working, reliable, I'm rarely afraid,
A soldier for years, electrician by trade,
Played in bands most my life, though was never a star,
But enjoyed every gig, playing my bass guitar,
And yes was in love, for nigh thirty years,
A fairy tale which, sadly ended in tears,
And my daughter God bless her, outspoken a tad,
She says I'm a special and really nice dad,
Though her comments admittedly carry some merit,
With the Hall Marks of someone who's due to inherit,
Oh, and regards the above, if you just didn't know it,
Sometimes I think of myself as a poet.

Verily 1st Earl of Runnymede

The Pessimist

(Another of those days when the author had little else to reflect on)

You know how minds can wander, sometimes your thoughts have
wings,
It's surprising how it's possible, to think the strangest things,
Perception too is everything, it varies day to day,
Ask a pessimist his comments, and I'm sure here's what he'd say. . . . . .
Comedians aren't funny, all they do is mocking,
And electricians if you ask me, are nothing less than shocking,
Designers, they are something else, and on a learning curve,
Neurologists are just as bad, they've really got some nerve,
Poisoners are awful, they really make me sick,
And Candle makers say they're nice, but still get on your wick,
Plasterers working everywhere, from Scotland down to Dover,
Never finish what they do, instead just smooth things over,
Surgeons only stitch you up, gardeners only mown,
And teachers one and all are in, a class all of their own,
Taxi drivers drive about, and say they've nowt to hide,
They charge you at the going rate, but still take you for a ride,
Farmers they are in I'm told, a field, of their own,
And butchers if you argue, they will cut you to the bone,
Police have double vision, they see two of you and so,
Every time one speaks to you he says Hello Hello,
And Wimbledon's no different, the players earn a packet,
They take advantage all the time, it's just another racket,
Singers charge a higher rate when singing at full throttle,
Milkmen cannot be that brave, and few of them have bottle,
Tailors are well suited, Church Ministers are meek,
And so, they should be, as they work for, just one day a week,
And poets, well what can I say, but sure you will agree,
Good looking, witty, charming, but get bored so easily.

Verily 1st Earl of Runnymede

My Menopause

Menopause can make you feel, like you are going mad
One minute you are happy, the next feel really sad.
Aches and pains, dry itchy skin, you feel that you can't win.
You feel annoyed and angry, how your hormones left you in.
Hot flushes, loss of sex drive, whatever else can be.
Oh yes, you've just remembered, your loss of sanity.
I'm told that things get better, take time out for yourself.
Calming meditation, can be good for mental health.
So, ladies stick together, it's good to talk you know.
We will beat these horrid symptoms, until they bloody go.

Dora Blandford

Pigs can Fly

(The author's sister has given up chocolate – or has she)

Since I've not received a phone call, or a letter of reply,
I'll assume I was correct when I predicted "Pigs can fly"
It's just that you and chocolate, have been having this affair,
If the moon was made of chocolate, well I'm sure we'd find you there,
If the ocean was milk chocolate, and you had a boat, I think,
You'd up the anchor, put to sea, and try to make it sink,
Even sex cannot compete as such, it only comes in second,
Compared to your friend chocolate, which is always first we reckoned,
If you'd been caught by the Gestapo, and they wanted you to sing,
They'd confiscate your chocolate and you'd tell them everything,
And as for when you dated boys, on your way home from a show,
If they ever brought you chocolates, well, I just don't want to know,
Unless of course I have been wrong, and I mean no offence,
When suggesting that you've finally, come to grips with abstinence,
That you've said farewell to Chocolate, and are coping with your fast,
Ooooops Guess what, another pig, has just gone flying past!

Verily 1st Earl of Runnymede

115

The Rose

(The author arranged for a rose and this verse to be left in someone's hotel room to cheer them up)

I imagine by now; you'll be speechless and more.
Maybe thinking you're dreaming, or really not sure,
But as you were so thoughtful, with that phone call of late,
To reciprocate I.... well I just couldn't wait,
And as good luck would have it, without so much as praying,
You told me the hotel, at which you were staying,
Information I played down, but none the less heeded,
And along with your surname, that was all that I needed,
In considering options, I've taken a chance,
But things would have been different, had I known in advance,
Would have given me pleasure, irrespective of price,
To have hidden some goodies, or arrange something nice,
But alas of surprises, of which I have spoken,
By comparison this, is but a mere token,
With good fortune I hope, you will see my intend,
This, although gesture small, has been sent by a friend,
With kind aims but whose options, were decidedly few,
As to what in the time scale, he could possibly do,
So, as you're down in Cornwall, and I am so far,
I've sent you a rose, for the rose that you are,
If it's caused you to smile, which I'm hoping and guess,
I'll consider my actions, a resounding success.

Verily 1st Earl of Runnymede

116

Watching Waters

(The author reflects)

I reflected at last, on the weekend just past,
Watching waters to me was a break,
Forest streams worth a look, tidal sea, and a brook,
Not forgetting a clear mountain lake,
But to see them alone, cools the heart to the bone,
And when viewed by oneself, they are duller,
Though a glorious sight, they are still black and white
Whereas friends being there can add colour.

And in so many ways, it's these such pleasant days,
On these journeys to coastlines and ports,
That occasions they lend, to an absent close friend,
Little wonder I'm so deep in thoughts,
Of the things I have done, which were once lots more fun,
And although watching waters is fine,
How I'd love the refrain, see those waters again,
With the one that I loved and called mine,

Verily 1st Earl of Runnymede

Taking the Pen Again

(The author attempts a few verses to his sister after a marked absence)

There were times I could write, there were times I saw fit, to combine
composition with sarcastic wit,
Whose verses when published, and I'd say more than half, in tease of a
victim produced a good laugh,
But whilst hosting a year, in which my tomorrow, expired in oceans, of
sadness and sorrow,
I found my good humour, this gift and this flair, fell a victim as such,
and was no longer there,
Till a letter received, the first one in weeks, containing a poem, brought
a smile to my cheeks,
Which inspired competition, and I thought I would try, for the first
time in ages, to attempt a reply.

There was plenty to write of, like the visit from you, and it has to be
said, it was long overdue,
It was nice to catch up on old chit chat for one, it was old memory lane
and a great deal of fun,
Apart from the nightmares, which came without warning, with my
bedroom door opening, at half three in the morning,
And in at the start, of this mind haunting dream, entered shuffling
pyjamas, enveloped in steam,
Coming closer a barrel shape, bone china cup, and a blood curdling
voice asking Why Aren't You Up?
But the strange thing is this, at the touch of a button, the ghost hasn't
returned, since you went back to Sutton.

Now regards Rugby Union, last weekend's premier fixture, between
England and Scotland, was described was a mixture,
At best using sport, to redress an old score, at worst Armageddon, and
the outbreak of war,

England took on the best, of the best of the Jocks, who dispensed with their kilts, but still wore tartan socks,
But it did them no good, for the Red English Rose, gave the Flower of Scotland, a deserved bloodied nose,
The Jocks got a drubbing, they were kicked into touch, which goes to point out, they've not learnt very much,
Though it's only a game, played on turf which is trodden, it proves nothing's changed, since the days of Culloden.

The children returned from their sporting weekend, bearing chocolates for dad and less money to spend,
Running and walking, swimming if they were able, they played games of tennis, with a ball on a table,
But they also ate out, and to diet endeavour, but returned back to Stone sadly, heavier than ever,
And it didn't stop there, as the dieting should, they returned to roast beef, and a large Yorkshire pud,
Poor Chris hurt his back, and was walking in pain, and arched his back stiffly, every now and again,
And I put my foot in it, when I said that for weeks, I thought that his shirt tails, had been caught in his cheeks.

Well that's all for now Sue, re mistakes I'm exempt, after months of long absence this is my first attempt,
It took quite some time, compared to before, it seems that my flair, pray has gone through the door,
Anne and Norman are coming, they'll be here pretty soon, arriving by coach, late this afternoon,
So, I better get moving, and finish this ditty, I've got to collect them from Manchester City,
With regards to your casual and much welcome visit, I just wanted to say, it was grand and exquisite,
And I'm hoping that soon, when you've no place to go, you'll come back to Stone, just to see me…Your Bro'

Verily 1st Earl of Runnymede

119

The Dying Garden

(October in the author's garden)

My poor old summer garden, methinks the end is near,
The flowers look so very tired, they sense the autumn's here,
My London's pride has lost its pride, it's leaves looks burnt and duller,
The Fuscias have all faded, and now lack all life and colour,
My Penstemons are all wilted, and lying on their side,
The Asters and the Daisies, like the Pansies have all died,
My Clematis has stopped climbing, and now gone off the boil,
And the place where I grew Marigolds, is now just barren soil,
My Lilacs now are only twigs, and they have nothing on,
My cherry tree has branches, but all the leaves have gone,
But my stately Pyracantha, it looks stunning, so is said,
A wall of berries ten feet high, each one a postal red,
It was Diana's favourite plant, it thus caused me much pain,
For I wish that she could see it, in its glory, once again.

Verily 1st Earl of Runnymede

A Favour

(And of course, it worked, and we became happily married)

Mrs Brown I've this notion, I've harboured of late,
To be holding some flowers, by your front garden gate,
There to burst into song, with my arms all awave,
Dressed to kill in a suit, wearing nice after shave,
Now forgive me for getting you hot and excited,
And the last thing I'd want, is for you to feel blighted,
But I'm asking a favour, hopefully in the right manner,
To pass on a message to your daughter Diana,
As I'm after a nice hand, to place inside mine
Will you ask her from me, to be my Valentine.

Verily 1st Earl of Runnymede

(The author was sitting with her daughter in a hospital department waiting to have an Endoscopy when a poem came to mind)

Sitting in the waiting room

Sitting in the waiting room everyone is quiet,
Nil by mouth from last night, as if you're on a diet.
Tummy is a churning of what may happen now,
They take you in a room, and you ask when and how.
It may be a bit uncomfortable but not to worry so,
The nurse will hold your hand, and tell you where to go.
Scopes can be very long and sometimes very thick.
They tickle you on the way down, and can even make you sick.
But once it is all over and everything is done,
you can go out into town, and have dinner with your mum.

Dora Blandford

The Pencil

(The author purchased a large pencil measuring over a foot in length for his friend)

As a loyal, gifted wise and trim, associate of mine,
I thought that I would mark the end, of 1999,
With a kind and fitting gesture, after all, you've been so good,
In supplying me with all my needs, like plaster, bricks and wood,
In truth reciprocation, for the pencils I've supplied,
But demand exceeded shipments, although I've really tried,
So, I searched the shops in earnest, and kept looking hard to find,
Until I found the ideal gift, that I had got in mind,
And I reckoned as I bought it, as a general rule of thumb,
If sharpened it should last you 'til. . . the third Millennium.!

Verily 1st Earl of Runnymede

Mrs Shelley's Spruce

(The author was cutting his laurel hedge, when a neighbour in jest, pointed to a lone twig I had missed, in similar friendly vein I allowed the twig to grow until it was very prominent, the said neighbour referred to it as her Spruce)

There are many types of monument, to look and to behold,
Some of those quite recent, and others very old,
Most of which are on a plinth, surrounded by a fence,
Commemorating martyrs, famous people and events,
But one is like gallows, though it hasn't got a noose,
It's found in Maple gardens, and that's Mrs Shelley's Spruce!

Churchill's statue is in London, as are most our heroes there,
Nelson standing proudly, high above Trafalgar Square,
The memorial to Tyndall, outside Bristol is to see,
He was guilty and was burned, they say for heresy,
And in Scotland there's a statue, depicting Rob the Bruce,
But none of these compares at all, to Mrs Shelley's Spruce!

Now this monument's quite special, to those up the street and me,
So, I've had to take precautions with regards security,
I keep a watch throughout the day, and for the winter nights,
I've fitted CCTV, and some automatic lights,
After all there's many thugs about and vandals on the loose,
And I wouldn't want it damaged done, to Mrs Shelley's Spruce!

Some think I should just snip it off, but others they just say,
Leave the twig another month, and then call it a day,
It's now become a talking point, the highlight of the street,
A compass point for ramblers, a place where mothers meet,
Some say it should be cut down, or put to better use,
But me I think it's better left, as Mrs Shelley's Spruce!

They say the feature came about, when comments came to rest,
Inflicting satire on a friend, which all were said in jest,
And reciprocating rightfully, a hedge became embossed,
Resulting in a gesture, with aims a good riposte,
It started and it ended with, a deed from Mother Goose,
That's why there is a monument, called Mrs Shelley's Spruce!

Was in neighbourly affection, and a good means to an end,
A laurel branch abandoned, by chance happened to offend,
The remaining hedge well angled, and trimmed so perfectly,
Leaving just a token twig, stuck up defiantly,
Is it time to get the secateurs, is it time to call a truce,
Or just accept the monument, called Mrs Shelley's Spruce!

Verily 1st Earl of Runnymede

125

A Job done in Tamworth

(The author does some work for his nephew)

I was thinking out loud, and was hastened to laugh,
When I thought of the ease, getting you out the bath,
With a rap and a tap on your door with much vigour,
Which produced from a window, a half-naked figure,
Was a system that worked, though the sight brought me pain,
Having vomited twice, I'll not do that again.

I was beckoned to entry, that got me impressed,
And I made us some tea while you got yourself dressed,
The water was able, the sugar was sweet,
But the tea bags contained, nothing stronger than peat,
Having stirred with a spoon, I then had to quit,
For it looked and it tasted, like warm weasel spit.

The girls had gone out, spending money downtown,
Was for us curtains off, bedding out, pictures down,
A check with the ruler, beats a stab in the dark,
So, we scribed the four walls, with a pencil to mark,
Then we cut and we "Stickied" in truth it was fun,
A clunk of the hammer and the coving was done.

By noon having sweated, ample calories burned,
Bearing dog food and doughnuts, the ladies returned,
And thankfully Sue, with motives so kind,
Made lunch with a vengeance, and my waistline in mind,
Greying hair, failing eyes, aching joints, piles too,
But believe me the appetite is as good as brand new.

Was my pleasure young RP, I was glad I could master,
And help put up coving and dollop some plaster,
When the next rooms are ready, the bathroom or hall,
I'll not keep you waiting, so give us a call,
Though the next time I'm bringing, and I hope you won't mind,
Some tea bags of mine, of a much stronger kind!

Verily 1st Earl of Runnymede

Cinderella

(The author, much to his horror, finds himself left off the
guest list to attend a family social function of note)

Was a hot and peaceful Saturday, the day eighteen of June,
As a social court was gathering, and not a mite too soon,
Arriving guests accepting, with their written yes's,
Men in stiff tuxedos, and the ladies evening dresses,
Greeted by, Pimm's number 5, prior chilled, with ice from fridge,
To wine and dine, from six 'till nine, outdoors on Acorn Ridge,
That is of course except one chap, a most unlucky fella,
An Uncle, very Old one, who is known as Cinderella.

There was lucid lamb, a stick kebab, on charcoal fire was laid,
Brought to a halt, with seasoned salt and Tikka marinade,
Mushroom buttons picked that day, by virgins hand indeed,
A treat when one considers, that they are so rare a breed,
Coleslaw by the spoonful, condiments on tap,
Wedgewood plates to eat from, and serviettes for lap,
Tomatoes from the Netherlands, peppers red and yella'
Was had by all the honoured guests, but no so Cinderella.

The second course delighted, a sight which made one sigh,
A segment sweet of Key lime, or Florida Orange Pie,
With glacés from the freezer, to cool the sole intent,
A choice of Cornish clotted cream, or juices compliment,
The third course less in grandeur, but no doubt served to please,
An echelon of crackers and a clause of cheddar cheese,
Palates moistened to perfection, with some claret from the cellar,
Was had by all the honoured guests, but not so Cinderella.

Who needs a pumpkin large enough, on that I'll have to pass,
Four white mice to pull the coach, or slippers made of glass,
Who needs a frog to leap out from, a murky shallow pond,
Or a fairy God mum brandishing, a proper magic wand,
Who needs a timepiece good enough, to show me what's the time,
And as it comes to midnight, should I listen for its chime,
I need them, that's who needs them, I'm that most unlucky fella,
Your Uncle, very Old who now, is known as Cinderella.

Verily 1st Earl of Runnymede

127

(The Authors thoughts about a new-born baby coming into the world)

A life

A life form grows, from a little embryo,
Inside a warm, and loving caring place.
Fed, watered, until fully grown,
for nine whole months unknown!

A dark channel, to come out through,
struggling it's hardest, to get to see you.
A push, a squeeze and a little tiny cry.
Relief! A baby lets out another sigh.

The love is felt, the emotions start.
This little life has a beating heart.
Cradled in arms and covered in love.
A new-born baby, to hold with kid gloves.
New beginnings and a new life.
A new start for a man and his wife.

Dora Blandford

The Christmas fairy

(The author's take on why a fairy is always placed on the top of a Christmas tree)

Santa left the north pole, exactly as he'd planned,
Arrived somewhere in England, and then came into land,
Poor Rudolph he was livid, as well as being froze,
For some merrymaking locals, made remarks about his nose,
Rudolph couldn't help his Red Nose, and took it as a snub,
For one said - Look there's Rudolph, on his way back from the Pub.

Uncle Holly gathered presents, he was working from a list,
But he'd drunk a lot of sherry and by now he was quite inebriated.
He passed them to the fairy, she piled them at the back,
Then Santa picked the lot up, and put them in his sack,
Uncle Holly said poor Santa, the sack he's got is whopping,
Methinks that someone from this house, has been out Christmas
shoppin.

Santa climbed the chimney, looking forward to his cuppa,
And began to look around to find, his mince pies and his supper,
He looked beside the fireplace, and although a plate was there,
The sherry glass was empty, and the plate itself was bare,
Santa got a cob on, said nothing and was quiet,
As Santa was so overweight, they'd put him on a diet.

And with that he left the presents, although Santa wasn't jolly,
Plus, some evergreen was left as well, that is, by Uncle Holly,
The fairy left a Christmas tree, but then said oh dear me,
And told Santa she'd mis-counted, that she had an extra tree,
She said what shall I do with it, I am a silly lass,
And Santa said for all I care; you can stick it up your loft.

Verily 1st Earl of Runnymede

England's had a chequered history, in the past one thousand years, And it's worth a recollection, as the final minute nears, Leif Ericsson the Viking after getting up to tricks, Took second place to William who arrived 1066, That's when poor Harold couldn't see, an arrow on the wing, And after it had come to rest, he couldn't see a thing, Now the Normans were no amateurs, they're worth another look, They brought with them the "Cul-de-Sac" and wrote the domesday book, Things settled down in general, but it's true mistakes were made, Like the war to take Jerusalem, they called it the Crusade, Four times they fought the infidels, to set the Christians free, It's true they won the first round but they lost the other three, At the same time Thomas Beckett, a man of pious wealth, Demonstrated how cathedrals could be hazardous to health, Then King Edward marched his army off to Harlech and to war, Defeating all the Welshmen, in late 1284, But after that the diplomats, they opted for a truce, The Scots they won at Bannockburn, all thanks to Mr Bruce, The black death came by rats in ships, in 1349, And the symptoms of a cold were then, seen as a fatal sign, If anybody had a sneeze, they soon began to pray, And the habit of a blessing, still continues to this day, Incredibly as it may seem in 1362, For the first time English language was official, and it's true, Now in the year 1401, the king he changed the rules, And decreed that all heretics could be used as fossil fuels, Some victims were defiant, and refused so much a spark, But not so when they set alight, the rebel Joan of Arc, John Caxton made the printing press, the best of all inventions, But unlike Robert Maxwell, he didn't steal the pensions, James the fourth fell at Flodden and in 1534, Supremacy, King over church, became an act of Law, King Henry ruled with iron fist but soon the strains were showing, It drove him mad the sound of 16 knitting needles going, Elizabeth the first was crowned, "My feeble frame" she said, Francis Drake was knighted, and Mary lost her head, And then the crowns of Scotland and of England were united, Looking back it shows the commons, must have been a bit short sighted, Guy Fawkes made the headlines next and featured in the news, Packed explosives into parliament, but forgot to light the fuse, In 1616 Shakespeare died but before he passed away, Proved it was unlucky, to quote "A Scottish Play" King Charles tried to arrest five squires, but someone locked the door, Parliament stood firm, and yes they won the civil war, That's when Cromwell wrote the warrant, and made all his partners sign, Before he cut the Kings head off, in 1649, Again the plague took England and it spread to London town, But at least this time, someone had the sense to burn in down, The Battle of the Boyne came next, the thorn in England's crutch, King Billy and the protestants, kicked King James into touch, For the Saxon it's now history, but the Irish don't forget, Four hundred years has passed and yet, we're still not speaking yet, The Bank of England came along the Chancellor to impress, So to in 1695 the freedom of the press, The Jacobites invaded, but soon they all retreated, At Culloden they met Cumberland and quickly were defeated, At Trafalgar Nelson beat the French with cannon, drums and pipers, His final words to Hardy was "I can't see any snipers" But that was naval action, there was war in Belgium too, Wellington met Bonaparte and fought at waterloo, That was in 1815, resulting it was reckoned, The Iron Duke had won the day, and Napoleon came second, Unions were then legalised, postal stamps then came, Nobody could write but still they bought them all the same, In 1894 they dug, a ship canal inland, Now it's full of bed ends but it wasn't what they planned, The Suffragettes they won the vote, Victoria passed away, Scott of the Antarctic, he took off with his sleigh, The Titanic put to sea but all the passengers were heated, They'd all bought two way tickets, and thought that they'd been cheated, Then war in 1914, England intervened by chance, Her sons they bled their youth away in Belgium and in France, With peace in 1918, Oxford bent its knees, For the first time letting ladies sit and read for their degrees, The general strike was dodgy, the workers got the hump, For there wasn't any jobs around, they said it was a slump, Germany got restless and used its military power, But under Winston Churchill, England had its finest hour, The troops returned victorious, but they'd been away too long, For nine months after dad got home that's when I came along, Inventions and technology were explosive that's a fact, Ask the Christmas island natives, if their hearing's still intact, Huge Golf balls could be seen in fields, their purpose early warning, Churchill died in 65, the nation went in mourning, England won the world cup, all thanks to Bobby Moore, It seems the Germans can't play football, and they weren't much good at war. Arthur Scargill led the miners' strike, the result could be expected, They couldn't hope to win while Mrs Thatcher was elected, The rest is recent history, there's no space to write it all, Apart from how for common sense the writing's on the wall, No church or grand Cathedral, or similar equation, Instead they built the Greenwich Dome to mark this great occasion, Yes I'm proud of mother England, she's been good to me and fun, But for the record I would like it known, she's not the only one, As the new Millennium shows its face, and as the old one meets it's end, I want to say how nice it's been… to have you as a **friend !**

Verily 1st Earl of Runnymede

About the Authors

Dora Blandford (AKA the crazy hedgehog lady)
Dora and her husband enjoy watching and feeding, the many
hedgehogs that come into their garden, on a regular basis.
She works for the NHS at her local hospital
Loves anything to do with nature, it's such a fascinating and wonderful
thing to enjoy..........

And then there's Verily, a man out to share his humorous take, on any
and all situations, he rarely takes offence, even less a gate! an
accomplished pen and sharp wit. His identity has never quite been
established although it's rumoured he's one of Dora's cousins.

Acknowledgments

(A little ditty from Dora to Verily)

While writing some poems, which were very few, while dreaming of making a book,
I called on my cousin to tell him the news, and asked if he'd care take a look,
I knew he wrote prose, about young and the old, and all of the Mickey he's took.
So, come on Verily, it's just you and me, we'll write our own poetry book!

Verily:.... you are a star! and we are so proud of your work, it's a great honour to have come together with you, to make this book happen.

A big thanks to those who have had a mention in this book, **you know who you are....**
A special thank you to Richard for all the help and support to edit and put our book together, without his help our book wouldn't have been possible, and we are truly grateful.

Printed in Great Britain
by Amazon